THE EAST-WEST CENTER, established in Hawaii by the United States Congress in 1960, is a national educational institution with multinational programs. Its purpose is to promote better relations and understanding among the nations and peoples of Asia, the Pacific area, and the United States through their cooperative participation in research, study and training activities.

Fundamental to the achievement of the Center's purpose is the cooperative discovery and application of knowledge, and the interchange of knowledge, information, ideas, and beliefs in an intercultural atmosphere of academic freedom. In Center programs, theory and practice are combined to help current and future leaders generate, test, and share knowledge about important world problems of mutual concern to people in both East and West.

Each year about 1500 scholars, leaders, public officials, mid-level and upper-level managers, and graduate students come to the Center to work and study together in programs concerned with seeking alternative approaches and solutions to common programs. For each participant from the United States, two come from the Asian/Pacific area. An international, interdisciplinary, professional staff provides the framework, content, and continuity for programs and for cooperative relationships with universities and other institutions in Center's area of operations.

Center programs are conducted by the East-West Communication Institute, the East-West Culture Learning Institute, the East-West Food Institute, the East-West Population Institute, and the East-West Technology and Development Institute. Each year the Center also awards a limited number of Open Grants for graduate degree education and research by scholars and authorities in areas not encompassed by the problem-oriented institutes.

The East-West Center is governed by the autonomous board of a public, nonprofit educational corporation—the Center for Cultural and Technical Interchange between East and West, Inc.—established by special act of the Hawaii State Legislature. The Board of Governors is composed of distinguished individuals from the United States and countries of Asia and the Pacific area. The United States Congress provides basic funding for Center programs and for a variety of scholarships, fellowships, internships, and other awards. Because of the cooperative nature of Center programs, financial support and cost-sharing arrangements also are provided by Asian and Pacific governments, regional agencies, private enterprise, and foundations.

The Center is located in Honolulu, Hawaii, on 21 acres of land adjacent to the University of Hawaii's Manoa campus. Through cooperative arrangements with the University of Hawaii, the Center has access to University degree programs, libraries, computer center, and the like.

THE EAST-WEST CULTURE LEARNING INSTITUTE seeks to develop more effective methods of helping persons from different cultures to understand other cultures as well as their own. In particular, the Institute is concerned with ways and means by which cultures may come in contact with each other for the mutual benefit of persons in those cultures while individual and national identities are maintained. For program purposes, it conducts cooperative research, study, and training in four main areas: cultural identity, language in culture, cultures in contact, and thought and expression in culture learning.

Verner C. Bickley, Director

Editorial Board:
Mark P. Lester, Chairman
J.G. Amirthanayagam
Jerry Boucher
Richard Brislin
Krishna Kumar
Larry Smith
Gregory Trifonovitch
John Walsh
Karen Watson-Gegeo
David Wu

ENGLISH IN
THREE ACTS

RICHARD A. VIA, a professional man of the theater for twenty-three years, presently is an assistant professor of English as a second language at the University of Hawaii, Manoa, and Visiting Researcher at the Culture Learning Institute, East-West Center.

Awarded a Fulbright scholarship in 1966, he spent the next two years lecturing in Japan on the American theater. He received a grant from the JDR III Foundation in 1969, and served as a researcher and advisor to the English Language Educational Council, Tokyo, Japan, during 1969 and 1970.

His previous publications include *Playing with English*, coauthored with Don Pomes (Tokyo: Kenkyusha, 1973), numerous journal articles, and plays.

ENGLISH IN THREE ACTS

Richard A. Via

A Culture Learning
Institute Monograph

EAST-WEST CENTER

THE UNIVERSITY PRESS OF HAWAII

Never on Wednesday was previously published in *Elec Bulletin*, no. 33,
Spring 1971, and *English Teaching Forum*, July-August 1972.
The Now was previously published in *Elec Bulletin*, no. 34, Summer 1971.
Garage Sale will be published in *English Teaching Forum*, January 1976.

Via, Richard A   1922–
    English in three acts.

    (A Culture Learning Institute monograph)
    Bibliography: p.
    1. English language—Study and teaching—Foreign
students. 2. Drama in education. I. Title.
II. Series: East-West Center. Culture Learning
Institute. A Culture Learning Institute monograph.
PE1128.V43   428′.007   75-35816
ISBN 0-8248-0380-9

.195260

First printing 1976
Second printing 1978

For the Students of Model Productions

CONTENTS

ILLUSTRATIONS

FOREWORD

Richard Via's approach to teaching English through drama first achieved widespread attention through the July-August 1972 issue of the *English Teaching Forum*, a journal published by the United States Information Agency. In addition to Via's article, "English through Drama," describing his approach, there also appeared in the same issue one of his classroom plays, *Never on Wednesday*, (which also appears herein), and an article by Floyd Cammack describing Via's approach to English teaching, "Language Learning via Via."

The use of drama to teach foreign languages is by no means new; however, what is new is Via's careful application of the techniques of teaching acting and dramatization to the classroom teaching of English. It is important to understand that Via is *not* proposing the staging of plays as an extracurricular adjunct to the regular English program for an elite of literature-oriented English students. Via's technique can be used by any class concerned with teaching oral English. The only restriction is that it is not a technique that could be used easily with absolute beginners. It can be used with small- or medium-sized classes, and could even be used in large classes, but with some loss of effectiveness, as with any other technique that teaches oral English.

Before discussing Via's approach, it might be useful to comment briefly on the general motivation for using drama in the language classroom. The great advantage of drama is that it allows the student to use natural, conversational English in a meaningful context. The interchanges between characters involve the establishment of personalities and motives so that in the persona of the character, the student has a genuine communication need that other classroom techniques seldom provide. Furthermore, the very fact that the student is given a persona allows him a special kind of freedom to express attitudes and feelings in English that he would be very reluctant to attempt on his own.

A second advantage of drama in language teaching is that a play demands that the actors participate in new cultural roles and behave in a culturally acceptable way. Playing a role demands that the actors develop a sensitivity to how English speakers interreact with each other—for example, how they hold their bodies, how far they stand apart, where they look when they talk, how men shake hands with each other, how children talk to their parents, and so on. It also demands a great awareness of the ordinary mechanics of daily life in English-speaking countries—for example, what time people have their meals, what they eat, the kind of clothing they wear at home, how much furniture a room would have and so on. Needless to say, these topics are seldom dealt with in the conventional language classroom, even those that focus on conversational English. A classroom that uses drama is not only concerned with the words and expressions that English speakers use, but with the situations in which the words and expressions should and should not be used.

A third advantage of drama in language teaching is that it provides a purposeful, highly motivating classroom activity for intermediate and advanced level students. The widely used techniques of drill and repetition of language patterns provide a highly controlled and structured experience for beginning students. However, as the student gains control of the basic vocabulary and structures of the second language he needs to explore their use in more natural ways if he is to gain any genuine fluency. Drama provides at least one practicable classroom technique for developing fluency in the second language by focusing on the communicative needs of characters in an actual meaningful situation. Drama is a purposeful activity because it gives the students something to do that has a beginning, and middle, and an end, even if the end is a performance before their own classmates. It is motivating because every participating student has a specific responsibility in making a group activity a success. There is a sense of participation in a team effort which makes the class into a very supportive self-motivating group.

What is unique about Via's approach to teaching English through drama is his emphasis on the need for a wide range of preparatory activities. For Via, the performance of a play is the end result of a lengthy learning experience by all the participants. The goal of this lengthy preparation is not perfection of a highly stylized form of talking and behaving on stage, but on the contrary, is a totally natural performance in which the actors appear to be behaving and talking in a spontaneously correct way for their roles.

I believe that one key to the success of Via's approach is fact that it is really double-barreled: the play provides one kind of exposure to the natural communicative use of language while the use of English in the preparation of the play provides a second kind. In order to talk, you have to talk about something. For Via, the play has the double function of being both an end in itself and a topic for discussion and analysis which is deeply involving to the participants.

The preparatory activities range from short, mechanical breathing exercises to the highly introspective exercises that assist the actor in growing into the character of his part. While the various activities have the overt purpose of preparing the students for their roles, they also serve a number of less obvious purposes. Some activities, like the breathing exercises for example, serve to make the students less self-conscious and help to develop a group feeling. They also serve to lessen the formal distance between the instructor and the students. Other activities serve to expand the student's awareness of the world around him. However, the important characteristics that most activities share is the need for the student to verbalize his own feelings and perceptions. Via's approach to putting on a play is to immerse the student in a series of activities that demand a rich verbal response.

One final point. The success of Via's approach is based on attention to detail in the preparation of a play. It is the detail that makes the performance seem natural and unaffected. It is the detail that captures the students' interest and provides the basis for their language enrichment. The goal of performance may loom so large in the minds of the students and the instructor that there may be a temptation to hurry through the preparatory stages. To do so would undercut the basic reason for doing the play in the first place: improving the students' ability to use oral English in a natural and situationally appropriate way.

MARK LESTER
Research Associate

Culture Learning Institute
East-West Center

ACKNOWLEDGMENTS

This book would not have been possible without the help of many friends and organizations. Perhaps by mentioning them here I can express in some small way my deep appreciation and gratitude to them. The East-West Culture Learning Institute, The JDR 3rd Fund, the Committee for the Cooperation on English in Japan, The Weatherhead Foundation, Tokyo American Culture Center, Verner Bickley, Richard Brislin, Ruth Crymes, Al Hoel, Randal Hongo Mark Lester, Christina Bratt Paulston, Ted Plaister, Don Pomes, Neal Scott, Datus Smith, Larry Smith, and Hazel Tatsuno. Thank you.

PROLOGUE

It never occurred to me that I would ever write a book concerned with teaching English. With the exception of a few recent journal articles, my writing has consisted of a number of occasionally produced one-act plays and an unproduced musical. (If the current trend in revivals and nostalgia continues perhaps it may yet see the light of the stage.)

Though I have been told repeatedly by my friends that I must plan my life to reach my goals, I have never been able to do it. It seems that I have allowed fate to control me, and certainly the fact that I became interested in language teaching happened quite by accident.

In early childhood I was bitten by the theatre bug. Why or how this happened I have never been able to discover, and though I tried to overcome this ridiculous notion at last I arrived in New York to become a star. Well, I didn't become a star, but I hung on for twenty-three years (I still pay union dues, for I still consider myself "in theatre") first as an actor, later as a stage manager and director.

Yes, theatre was exciting—it was fun to have dinner with Mary Martin, a midnight snack with Anne Bancroft, to dance with Suzanne Plachette, to discuss Shakespeare with Helen Hayes, to know Charlton Heston, Sada Thompson, Marlon Brando, Maureen Stapleton, and Tony Perkins *before* they made it. But, it is not as exciting, rewarding, fulfilling, meaningful (are these the terms?) as working with a group of Japanese university students, watching them learn English, Western culture, and develop their personalities by performing in a play.

One day while I was working with Steve Lawrence on *What Makes Sammy Run*, I received a phone call from Mary Martin asking me if I would like to join her as a stage manager on the State Department tour of *Hello Dolly*. The tour was to include Japan, Hong Kong, and Russia; after thinking it over a full two seconds, I accepted. The story of that tour could be another book, especially since Hong Kong and Russia were replaced by Viet Nam, Okinawa, and Korea.

PROLOGUE

Our reception in Tokyo was tremendous. We were in demand to appear here, go there, and this is precisely what we did to fulfill our cultural exchange duties. As part of this, the American Cultural Center in Tokyo requested four of us meet with a group of Japanese people interested in drama in a panel discussion. I was among those chosen and, three minutes before entering the room, was informed that I was to give a short talk on the history of the American musical. (This was a good introduction to cultural behavior in Japan as this type of experience happened often after I returned in 1966.) After my history lesson, the floor was opened up for discussion and the questions and answers began to fly. At the conclusion of this, there was an informal reception and each of us was surrounded by young people, who were asking questions about acting and Western culture. Their lack of knowledge of Western culture and acting styles was dismaying, and I realized that they were in need of someone to help them.

One young director, working on Thornton Wilder's *Our Town*, asked me what Americans ate for breakfast. Was he serious? Certainly everyone must know that we have bacon and eggs, orange juice, toast and coffee. (An hour or so later it dawned on me that I had no idea what a Japanese ate for breakfast, *I* had a great deal to learn, too.) After listening to and trying to answer many such questions as this, I wondered if it were not possible for someone at the U.S. Embassy to handle these questions. (How naive I was about what the Embassy would and would not do.)

I suppose my family background (my father is a Methodist minister) overcame me and something like the missionary zeal urged me to do something. I felt that perhaps this was the opportunity for me to do something important, for at times stage managing seemed an unrewarding and useless job. (Please take note of the "at times"—a show without good stage management is in serious trouble.)

Rather than go to Las Vegas with the show I applied for a Fulbright Scholarship which started a barrage of letters and cables to be sent and papers to be filled out in triplicate and filed. During the winter and spring when I could have been banking the extra money doled out by the sponsors of *Hello Dolly*, I went on the road with the Hungarian National Ballet. It was a good initiation for what was to come—trying to communicate with one hundred and ten mad, wonderful, and talented singers, dancers, and musicians who spoke no English. Here, "body talk" came in most handy as a means of communication.

So, nine months after my decision to teach, I arrived in Tokyo ready to open the doors of Western theatre to the uninformed student actors. Now, came the real surprise and shocker—I discovered that one does not study theatre in a Japanese university. There are a few scattered courses on Japanese theatre history and Western plays as literature, but no concentrated effort to prepare students for the professional theatre. Students who plan to go into the theatre must pass an examination and be accepted by a theatre company which then takes them on as an apprentice for two or three years. This meant that there was no "home" for me at a university. The outcome was that I was told that since I had the grant and was there, I should create a program. I set about to locate that group of two hundred "drama students" who had attended the panel discussion the day "I had seen the light." The drama students, or at least a portion of them, were assembled. It was then that I discovered their majors—law, economics, American literature, chemical engineering, etc. Their interest in drama was only an attempt to learn English, and their attendance at my lecture was to test their comprehension. At last their lack of knowledge of Western acting was explained. For fear that someone might be offended, there *are* many professional Japanese actors, directors, and technicians who have studied in the West and *do* understand our drama and techniques.

Within a week I was off to a university to observe a rehearsal of Eugene O'Neill's *Where the Cross Is Made*. The melodramatic overacting and posturing were as hard to imagine as what they were saying was to comprehend. I took copious notes and explained to the actors very carefully after the rehearsal. There were smiles of agreement at each thing I said and a joyous "thank you very much" at my departure. I promised them a return visit the next week.

At the next meeting they greeted me eagerly and ushered me into the rehearsal classroom and began rehearsing immediately. To my utter amazement and annoyance, nothing had changed. Every note and suggestion had been ignored. Was this their way of telling me, "Listen, *gaijin* (foreigner), we don't need your advice; we know what we're doing."? Again, I made notes (in most cases the same ones). When the discussion began, I asked why they had not done it the way I suggested a week before. At last, I had the answer. They had not understood one word (oh, maybe one word) that I had said and were too embarrassed to let me know they did not and too polite to stop me. It was a long and painful process to make my points clear and some things could not be changed, for they had been pounded in by repetition during the five months of rehearsals they had gone through preparing for the November drama contest. As I went to other universities, I found varying degrees of the same situation. I spent a great deal of time on subways, buses, trains, and in taxis trying to get to the eleven universities that I assisted that fall.

Through watching their rehearsals and talking with these students, I realized that to really help I would have had to have been there from the beginning to get them started on the right track. It also seemed that the methods generally used in our acting classes and in Broadway rehearsals would be most beneficial in learning language, too.

After many lectures and workshops on how to present a play, a student, Yoshimi Sekikawa, asked if I would direct a play using a student cast of students from different universities. As well as I can remember, I agreed immediately, for it meant that I could reach more schools and do more concentrated work. The students could then teach this method to their peers when the participants returned to their respective schools.

Thus, in the summer of 1967, Model Productions (MP) was born. It became our laboratory to experiment with many things over the next four years. We presented five full-length plays (*Picnic, Our Town, You Can't Take It With You, Curious Savage,* and *I Remember Mama*) with full productions. There were also fifteen one-act plays presented as they might be done in a classroom. The reaction of nearly four hundred participants and over 14,000 observers was overwhelming.

Overwhelming is not too strong a word to use in this case. Students were *using* English not *learning* English. The observers (the audiences at rehearsals and performances) were surprised that they understood the plays with their limited English. They understood because they saw communication on stage fitting into natural behavior in the proper cultural environment, rather than a recitation.

ACT I

WHY USE THE DRAMA METHOD?

"Drama is human beings confronted by situations which change them because of what they must face in dealing with those challenges."

Dorothy Heathcote
Improvisation
English In Education,
vol. 1, no. 8

"We learn through experience and experiencing, and no one teaches anyone anything."

Viola Spolin
Improvisation for the Theater

Language teachers are constantly searching for new ways to teach and to improve their teaching methods. Every few years the emphasis seems to shift on what is considered to be the most effective way of language teaching. I will stay out of this area altogether by stating that the drama method is not intended as the end-all solution. It is not a complete course in itself, but something to add to and enhance your language program.

By its very nature it is obvious that the drama method is aimed at conversation. Generally, the students I worked with were at an inter-mediate level in English learning. Unless you and your students have all the time in the world, it is necessary that your students have some basic language skills before attempting to use this method. An exception may be the use of creative drama with very young students.

A well-chosen play is a good model of spoken English. A successful playwright must be able to produce natural speech in proper context. He is not concerned with the rules and regulations of English, pattern practice, or in illustrating a particular structure, but in expressing ideas and feelings. In most cases the plays use the type of language in use in daily conversation, which is the type of dialogue that your students will find most useful.

It is a generally accepted fact that a language must be linked with all other aspects of a culture and that it is virtually impossible to learn a language fluently, independent of its cultural context. Yet this is not what is happening in many language classrooms. Students and teachers alike are struggling through vocabulary and grammatical rules ignoring the fact that unless they fit them into thinking, feeling, believing and behavior of the culture they will not fully understand the language.

A play can give us a good picture of language in its socio-cultural environment and show us how the situation affects the language. A play often demonstrates the interaction of many characters and illustrates the various levels of speech. If a teacher fails to introduce cultural knowledge into the classroom, the students are in danger of being trapped into interpreting the new language through their own cultural understanding.

A play is written for communication between actor and actor and audience and actor. The drama method offers a chance for the students to use and understand the language from the gut level. They can become involved in the situation and discover the how and why of the language. They are learning through the experience of communicating in the language; thus, their understanding of the language is greatly enhanced. My own students who have traveled out of Japan have had little or no culture shock. Through their drama experience they had already experienced many aspects of the new culture. They had learned to use English for all communication. The drama method can give students the confidence in the classroom that they will need outside.

The preceding points perhaps can best be summed up by a letter which a Japanese university girl wrote to her teacher after her first encounter with a play in English. "The drama class experience was the first time I realized that English *did* have meaning as a spoken language." Quite a statement, especially when you consider the fact that she had been studying English for eight years!

A play can give students a reason to use the language. Students generally feel that it is artificial or showoffish to speak English when others are within earshot. If the "English only" rule is adhered to in the classroom, then the play and all discussion about the play will become a logical situation in which to use English. English then becomes the tool it is intended to be. If it is announced at the beginning of the course that the play will be performed on a given date, the students will have a goal to reach. Students with a definite, interesting goal progress faster and further.

"On the night of June 5th we will perform a play in English," is much more helpful than, "learn as much English as you can by June 5th." Specific goals lead to higher performance than general goals.

Rehearsing and presenting a play is fun. When students are enjoying themselves and using a new language, they make the language " theirs," and are well on the way to mastering it. It was rare for me to ever get involved in a discussion about any of the technical aspects of language, or the rules and logic involved. In no way am I suggesting that we do away with this aspect of language training, for it is vital, but I do suggest that, during the time allotted to drama, it be curtailed. All emphasis should be placed on the play and its production. The threat that students often feel in language classes is removed, and the freedom gained sparks enjoyment, which will motivate them and encourage them to continue to use and study English.

Everyone likes to succeed. Look back at your past experiences, and you will realize how very important your successes were to you. More than likely after each success there were other successes soon after, and through it all, important learning took place. I asked a group of young Japanese businessmen if any of them had ever appeared in a play. A number of them had, but the surprising thing was that the performances took place when they were between five to eight years old. Yet, the experience had been a memorable one for them, so important in fact, that they could still remember lines, and minute details of the various productions. Nearly everyone enjoys acting. Oh, we put up protests about getting on stage, but deep down have we not all dreamed at one time or another of seeing our name in lights? Most of your students have the same desire, and a chance to act, to be up front, to show their friends what they can do, is a hidden desire.

In George Kelly's play, *The Flattering Word*, one of the characters says this, "Tell any man, woman or child that he should be on the stage,—and you'll find him quite as susceptible as a cat to catnip.... Because every human being has, at some time or other in his life, experienced the desire to be on the stage. Of course, he may not admit it; but he has, just the same; and if he hasn't, all you have got to do is tell him he should be on the stage, and he *will* experience it. I tell you Mary, that is the most universal susceptibility. And very naturally so; the most fundamental instinct of human life is to express oneself; and the stage is perhaps the most complete form of self expression; so that when a person is stage-struck he is simply struck with the desire to express himself more completely."

7

ACT I

To perform in a play is success. The satisfaction of the accomplishment of performing in a play in a foreign language is tremendous. In fact, most students will find joy in repeating the performance as often as possible for anyone who will watch. I have not known of a single group studying language this way that did not want to start work on another play as soon as they finished their first one.

Perhaps the most common remark made to me about the drama method and the reason others give for not using it is, "*You* can do it. You have the personality and the training, but I could never do it. I don't know anything about drama."

Let's tackle the first part of that statement—"special personality."Yes, I have a very special personality, but then doesn't everyone? Are you hiding behind a "teacher personality" that every one of your students recognizes as such? Have you dared to reveal your true self to your students? Delightful, humorous men and women often turn into dull and listless automatons when they stand in front of a group of students. Others are on the opposite side of the fence. They become sullen and uncommunicative in the teachers' room, but are overly solicitous to the students. More than likely the overly solicitous ones want to be loved so much that they are afraid of offending anyone. Students see through this. Oh, they will play the game, but they are not fooled.

If we are going to succeed and be happy in our work, rather than spending our lives waiting for the bell to ring to free us, we must get back to being one personality in all situations. Many of the activities discussed in this book, which, hopefully, you will be doing with your students, will aid you in becoming "one" person as well as teaching your students.

A word of warning. This is not a cookbook with simple one, two, three instructions for instant success. It is a book that is like a play with one character missing and that character is the star—you. You with all of your charm, quirks, hang-ups, shyness, and boisterous laughter must star in the application of this book. "Let it all hang out" as my good friend says, and you will find a new you, as well as find that your students suddenly find the language class the most exciting, meaningful, and rewarding (are they the words?) they have.

There is a point that should be brought up right here. Answer these questions honestly. Do you like students and do you like teaching a foreign language? If you have answered "yes" to one question, continue reading for you will be greatly rewarded. If you have answered "yes" to both questions, look out! You might set the world on fire. If you answered "no" to both questions close the book and rush to your bookstore for a refund. The dealer won't be able to tell you've read this far, so you can save a few bucks.

8

Now that you have passed the first examination and have decided to become the real you, perhaps this famous excerpt from Margery Williams, *The Velveteen Rabbit* will help you to realize your goal.

"What is real?" asked the rabbit one day, when they were lying side by side. "Does it mean having things that buzz inside you, and a stick-out handle?"

"Real isn't how you are made," said the skin horse. "It's a thing that happens to you. When a child loves you for a long, long time, not just to play with, but really loves you, then you become real."

"Does it hurt?" asked the rabbit.

"Sometimes," said the skin horse, for he was always truthful. "When you are real, you don't mind being hurt."

"Does it happen all at once, like being wound up, or bit by bit?"

"It doesn't happen all at once. You become. It takes a long time. That's why it doesn't happen often to people who break easily or have sharp edges, or have to be carefully kept. Generally, by the time you are real, most of your hair has been loved off, and your eyes drop out. And you get loose at the joints. But these things don't matter at all. Because once you are real, you can't be ugly. Except to people who don't understand."

Now for the second part of the sentence given earlier, "I could never do it, I don't know anything about drama." Balderdash! You pass judgment on numerous films, T.V. shows and books—you select what you like. One of the most important jobs of a director is selection—the actor brings his ideas to rehearsal and the director selects those that are most suitable. This book will give you exercises and instructions on freeing your students (and you) and helping them regain their natural creativity. No one expects you to be an Arthur Penn, Elia Kazan, or Alfred Hitchcock, or your students to perform like Anne Bancroft or Paul Newman. You are not conducting an acting class (though it will be better than many, I feel sure), but a language class. Again, let me warn you, however, that you will see performances that will amaze you—they will make you weep with their sensitiveness and roar with their naturalness, and your cohorts will urge you to give up teaching and show your talent to the world. Don't go! Stay in the classroom. You have found the magic that makes those exams, reports, and PTA meetings bearable. Yes, you can do it by using this book as a guide and starring the real you.

THE PROBLEMS

Yes, you will have problems in using the drama method, but they are not the problems you are thinking about right now. If my guess is correct, and from talking with teachers who were being instructed in the drama method, I think it is, you are worried about the following: (1) I don't know anything about the theater or about directing; (2) My students know nothing of acting; (3) What about rehearsal space? We don't have an auditorium; (4) We can't afford scenery and we wouldn't know how to build it if we could; (5) We'd never get an audience; (6) Where do I find plays?; and (7) I have forty students in my class.

Relax. This book will offer solutions to all of these, so they are not problems. Your problems will be the little unexpected things that happen everyday in your classroom that you manage to solve or choose to ignore.

To ease your worry about the seven "problems" above, let me discuss them in order.

1. I don't know anything about the theater... If you were an expert director or theater authority, you probably would not be teaching English and I could not sell this book to you. Remember too the aim is not to develop actors, but to aid in culture and language learning and to give your students confidence, so that they may increase their language flow and vocabulary growth.

2. My students know nothing of acting. Everyone can act. Everyone has creative ability within him and once he is freed from his anxieties or self-consciousness, can do wondrous things before an audience. Unobserved children at play often give Academy Award winning performances—they are uninhibited and are communicating with each other. Since we all were children at one time, we still have this ability. We must rediscover it.

3. What about rehearsal space? Perhaps this book should have been titled *Classroom Drama*, since for most of you the classroom will be your rehearsal hall and auditorium. (If, however, you have a large room or auditorium available to you, all the better.) The new look in theater as expressed in off-off Broadway or in Grotowskis' poor theater is to use the available space.

4. We can't afford scenery... Scenery? It's nice to have a wonderful set, but the traditional theatre of the past such as the Shakespearean and the Italian commedia used little if any scenery, and today there are countless theatres in the round that do not use scenery. Asian traditional theater often does not use scenery, and Thornton Wilder did away with scenery in several of his best works. The students and the audience are most imaginative and will create better scenery in their minds than you could ever provide. This also makes the audience active participants in the production.

5. We'd never get an audience. There is always an audience. The other students in the class; the ones who are not "on stage" at the moment, or the class in the next room (even if they are not studying English), and

10

of course, parents and family can be the audience. Many of the classroom drama projects done in Tokyo had standing room only; others had an audience of ten. I saw no difference in the joy of performing on the part of the actors.

6. *Where do I find plays?* There are seven plays in this book to use as starters, plus a list of recommended plays, and addresses of bookstores and publishing houses that can help you.

7. *I have forty students in my class.* This may appear to be the most difficult problem of all since most of the plays will only need five to ten performers. It is natural to wonder what to do with the other thirty students. I am not trying to complicate your teaching situation by suggesting that instead of doing one play, you do four. You may do four productions of the same play, but students are likely to compare, compete, and copy. Therefore, choose four different plays.

Select a "director" for each group. Perhaps the first reading should be done with everyone listening in on each play. At this time, you may help with pronunciation and any necessary explanations. After this, let them work by themselves in different areas of the room. You, the master director, will move from one group to another to help. When you are not with a group, be available in case you are needed.

In case you don't feel equal to doing four plays at once, you may try double and triple casting (using two or three students for each role). All of the students would participate in all of the warm-up and acting exercises. The students who are watching their fellow students perform during the actual rehearsal will be involved with what is going on. Your students know you can speak English and may be tired of your voice, but they will be interested in what other students can do. Though they are not up front "doing" they are participating by listening, (comprehension is a major element in the ability to take part in a conversation), and thinking of what they would do, or what the action should be in the situation.

Preliminary Activities

Give the students the rules of this new conversation class.

1. Once you enter the room you may speak only in English.

2. You must do anything the teacher/director asks you to do. (The director will not ask you to do anything that he/she will not do.)

3. Since this is a group project regular and on-time attendance is absolutely necessary.

4. You must be prepared to enjoy the class. You may talk or laugh whenever you wish.

On many occasions I had these rules mimeographed and asked the students to sign them. My main purpose in this was to strengthen rule number one. That's the important rule for your purposes. Most of your students will probably be happy and excited about this new approach to English conversation. There are unfortunately those who will take a "prove it" or "show me" attitude. It will be your job to win them over and prove it or show them. You can.

The arrangement of the classroom is very important. If you are in a regular classroom, you might have the students move the desks and/or tables and chairs the way you want them. This forces the students to work together and all of the language used should be English. Listen carefully and if they are using anything else, call it to their attention. Let them know you have magic ears that pick up these "strange sounds."

The other approach is to have the room arranged before the students arrive. Immediately they sense that something is different from the regular classroom. I readily admit that I have no preference between these two approaches. The way you arrange the desks and/or tables is completely up to you and may depend on what you want to do that day. If the room is large enough (which was rare in Japan), I liked to have a group of tables pushed together with seats enough for everyone to sit around the tables. Eventually you will need some open space even if it is only the four or five feet up front in a regular classroom. Sometimes I like to work with everyone sitting on the floor, but other times I place the desks or chairs in a circle.

VOICE

To prevent any misunderstanding on this let me assure you that I do not advocate a stage voice or perfect diction or standard English. The first is artificial, and the other two do not exist, or are in such great variety that who is to decide which is the right one.

Voice exercises can help students to project their own voices. The first duty of an actor and a conversationalist is that they be heard. In many cultures girls are taught that a loud voice is undesirable, not ladylike, and will be a deterrent to a suitable marriage. What is the poor girl to do, but to tone down and start whispering her way through life? What are shy students to do when they are confronted with English, which is a loud language, and discover that all teachers of English, as well as all Westerners, are deaf, they need help. The answer—voice lessons.

The paragraph above is to be used to answer your students' questions about the need of voice exercises. Now I'll tell you the real reason they are so important—relaxation and security! To begin speaking in a foreign language is a frightening experience. I know of teachers who greet their students with variations of the following: "English is a very difficult language, and you must study very hard, and even then you probably will do poorly. You must continue your study for years, or even your entire life." That kind of "greeting" is enough to kill any interest the student may have. To learn any language does require work, and there is no magic formula, but there are ways to take out the fear. The breathing and voice exercises are things that everyone can do without fear of making a mistake. The English that you use to describe the exercises should be simple, and together with the demonstration involved, the students will be able to follow you. Immediate success! The students have a small taste of security, for they *can* comprehend English.

In many of the martial arts of the East, such as kung-fu, judo, and karate, a yell accompanies the strike. This is not to frighten the opponent, but to build the confidence and increase the energy of the attacker. This same psychology holds true for language learners, a strong clear voice will give them confidence. The very sound of a weak voice and a weak body stance will discourage them.

Have your students stand with space on all sides. I prefer a circle so that I become a member of the group; others may prefer to be up front in order to be able to see all of their students.

I use two breathing exercises. I prefer the first one, but use the second when there is a space problem.

Breathing Exercises

1. Bend over hands to the toes, or as close as possible, and exhale all air.
2. Stand up, take a long slow breath filling the lungs as much as possible.
3. With teeth lightly pressed together and lips smiling exhale slowly making a humming z sound. Be sure to push from the diaphragm.
4. Continue this z sound until you have expelled all of the air. Do not cave in and bend the shoulders over to squeeze out the last bit of air. This only cuts the air off (as does hunching the shoulders up when inhaling). When you run out of steam, stop.
5. Repeat this several times and ask the students to practice it at free times.

The second is much simpler:
1. Expel all air.
2. Inhale slowly as you count to ten.
3. Hold your breath for about ten seconds.
4. Exhale as you continue your count to twenty.
Everyone should count in English. Repeat. Increase your count to 11–22, 12–24, etc. Again, you will want to push from the diaphragm.

Voice Exercises

1. Take a deep breath and exhale making a humming e–e–e sound. The mouth should be in the same position as for the *z* breathing sound, but e should be vocalized. E–e–e–e–e–e. Push the sound out of the top of the head. Of course, you cannot push a sound out of the top of the head, but it will help students to use the cavities of the head as a sounding board. It should give a deeper humming sound. You may feel the slight vibrations on the side of your nose.

2. Start with the e–e–e–e sound and go into an ah-h-h-h sound, letting the jaw drop naturally. Don't stretch or let the mouth spread sideways unnaturally.

3. Now add the *Oh* sound. Start again with e–e–e, then pursing the lips in a circle, make an oh sound, then drop the jaw to ah.

Repeat these exercises several times.

In all of these exercises, let the lips do a lot of exaggerated work to help the students discover the muscles that are now working automatically.

Before continuing with the voice exercises, this might be a good place to introduce the lip and tongue exercises since in a foreign language our lips and tongues must work in different ways. I am not of the school of showing exactly how the tongue and lips behave when pronouncing a new word. I prefer to let the students hear it and try to repeat it. If the mind is concerned with controlling the muscles of the tongue and lips, surely they will not be able to give the proper pronunciation. The lip and tongue exercises are meant to help them relax, thus, making it easier for them to reproduce the correct sound.

The Lip Exercise

1. Push the lips as far out as possible, making an *o* shape.
2. Pull them back over the teeth as far as possible.
3. Go back and forth between these two movements. Perhaps the young ladies of the group won't want to do this for it is not very pretty, but remind them of their agreement to follow the rules of the class.
4. Now, relax the lips and push air out making a sound like a motorboat or car. Nearly every child does this as he pushes his toy truck about the room or holds a tiny airplane making it "fly" about.

The Tongue Exercise

With the lips apart and the teeth together, let the tongue make rapid vibrations against the roof of the mouth just behind the teeth. It is possible to do this rather quietly, but I much prefer to make a sound like that of an air hammer.

Both of these exercises will cause a great deal of laughter and make everyone feel rather foolish, but equality is setting in. You are on your way to a relaxed classroom. But first, more voice exercises.

Rather than using just the vowel sound, as a singer might, add a consonant that may be a difficult sound for the student. For example, in Japan and many parts of Asia, one would add *l, r, f, w,* and the ever troublesome *th,* for example, *la, re, fo, wu, po,* and *the.*

With one of the combinations do the following exercise.

1. Take a deep breath and sing an arpeggio, that is the tones of a major chord.
2. Hold the top note for three counts.
3. Come back down.

Obviously there are hundreds of combinations to be used and it is easy for the teacher to observe the students and see if they are making the correct sound. Do not worry if the students are not making beautiful round, full tones; you are not training singers. Another way to use these exercises is to start them softly and let the loudest sound be the last; this will also aid the student in breath control.

After you have led the exercises for several days, have your students take over. Each one choosing the exercises he wishes to do. They now are using the new language to communicate with others. Warning: Don't let them select and then depend on you to lead. Wait for them to lead and follow their instructions even if they are wrong, like "let all the air out—bend over—up—e–e–e–e." They will soon discover that something is wrong and there is no air to make the sound. Someone will probably come to their aid if they don't figure it out for themselves. The important thing is that the new language is being used.

Voice and breathing exercises get your students in the habit of projecting. They will automatically use this later. Speaking in a stronger voice will give the students confidence in themselves, and their ability to use the new language. Kendo (Japanese fencing) has used a similar theory for years—a loud sound accompanies a strike, thus, giving the fencer more power and courage.

If you find that your group is a harmonious one and they are very relaxed, you may want to cut the voice exercises short to spend more time on other activities. If you should be conducting your class later in the afternoon or evening, you will find that the voice exercises are a great way of letting people relax and unwind. Since a good deal of my work in Japan was extracurricular and students were tired when they arrived for the drama program, I found the voice and relaxing exercises (described later) most refreshing for them. I used them at the start of every meeting.

Body Talk

An interesting activity to help students "open up," relax and to use their bodies to express ideas, is "body talk." It will also show students with a limited vocabulary that by using their bodies they can express many more thoughts. The whole class can participate in body talk at the same time giving you and them a chance to see the variety of ways people express the same thing. It is a good exercise for shy students for they are participating in a group activity and will feel more secure. You may notice, too, that the very shy will tend to follow or copy others. Do not make comments or worry about it because as the student becomes more secure this habit will disappear.

Ask your students to express the following ideas without using any words or sounds:

1. Hello.
2. It's cold today.
3. There's a bug on the ceiling.
4. The floor is hot.
5. I'm tired.

Of course, you or your students may think up others. One word of caution; when the students express "cold" ask them to remember how they really behave rather then indicating cold.

If you wish to take body talk two steps further, have them add sounds to the same ideas, and then have them add words. What sounds (not words) might be added to the body talk expressing, "It's cold today" to make it more colorful. When adding words, of course there are many ways of saying each idea. To the body talk of "Hello" one might say: "Hi," "How are you," "Good morning," "Good afternoon," "Good evening," and "Hello."

TALK AND LISTEN

Stanislavski saw that, probably because of the artificial atmosphere of the stage, in front of a mass of people an actor's senses are often prone to paralysis. The actor then loses the feeling of real life and forgets how to do the simplest things that he does naturally and spontaneously in life. Stanislavski realized that an actor has to learn anew to see and not just to pretend to see, to hear and not just to pretend to listen, that he has to talk to his fellow actors and not just to read lines, that he has to think and feel.

Sonia Moore
The Stanislavski System

How many students of English as a second language go through the same kind of paralysis mentioned above? The "Talk and Listen" system will help overcome this problem by helping students to relate to each other. In addition, it will eliminate a great deal of memory work. A common comment to amateur and professional actors is, "How did you memorize all those lines?" In language texts there are constant directions to "memorize the useful phrases below" or to "memorize these dialogues." In a message to students who were performing a play to learn English, a leading educator recommended modern plays because students could learn modern colloquial English by reciting the dialogues.

My challenge to you is to toss out the words "memorize" and "recite." Through memorization and recitation students have been misled into believing they could speak a language. Armed with the pat phrases learned by rote, students set out to practice their conversation on unsuspecting native speakers of English. The words come tumbling out at rapid speed ("I'm speaking like a native speaker," they think), and all meaning and true communication are lost. The native speaker is baffled by the outburst, and perhaps wonders if the rapid-fire recitation was an attempt at communication. The student in turn is baffled because the foreigner did not give the proper response, the response given in the memorized dialogue. Most students will then mumble an apology in their native language and flee realizing they are unable to speak another language, and vowing never to try again. It will be a difficult job to bring them back.

There is hope, though, for the students who barrel ahead undaunted by the experience and continue with their recitation. They have been trained to speak, not to listen, and nothing will stop them. To these students, conversation is speaking only and there are thousands of these robots roaming the world ready to pounce upon some innocent native speaker. Yes, there is hope for them, but they are in for some hard times, some insults, and hopefully a punch in the nose as someone shouts at them, "LISTEN!"

The picture is really not so overdrawn as it may seem. I have experienced both situations and since I am "in the business" I honestly tried to understand and be helpful. I must admit that I pitied the ones who gave up, and usually got very annoyed with the brave or obstinate ones who were going to say their piece, or else.

Even more annoying than the dialogue-practicing-sentence-memorizers, are the eager beavers who memorize a pocketful of handy idioms for every situation. They come on strong with their colloquial jargon hardly stopping for a breath, let alone a chance for you to speak. The few comments that you manage to squeeze in are ignored because they are not understood, and the student departs with a loud "see ya round" or one or another pat phrases convinced that they have impressed a foreigner with their language ability.

A native-speaker actor may be able to memorize lines and make them sound like conversation, but it's a difficult task. Do you remember the last amateur theatrical you saw? Were the actors reciting lines, or did you feel they were really talking to each other? Were you interested in the words that the playwright had written, or were you emotionally involved with the people on the stage?

Here is a simple and very obvious observation—conversation is not recitation, but communication.

Not all actors and Broadway directors subscribe to the "talk-and-listen" system, but it is used by a number of the leading players. I had watched its use during my early years in New York and had my doubts about its validity, but I am now a complete convert. I do know that it was most effective in Japan, and that most students felt it was the most important innovation that the drama method introduced. Students from the start are taught to communicate, rather than "seeing" the page in their minds, and reciting. They are taught to listen rather than to plan their next speech. This is a habit that should be developed early as an aid for the students to communicate, and for the enjoyment of the people they will be communicating with in the future.

The system is exactly what it says it is—*to talk* to people and *to listen* to people. Surely you have observed that your students who were reciting a dialogue by rote were not listening to what was said to them, for they were planning their next speech to be sure it was correct. Perhaps it has happened to you when learning another language. The students (or actors) who do not follow the talk-and-listen system are missing out on so much that would be of valuable help to them. The way things are said frequently controls the way a person replies as well as controlling the intonation and stress of the reply. Also often there are many parts of the sentence spoken which can be picked up to be used in a reply. By listening to others it is possible to enlarge one's vocabulary. In the context of the whole situation it is often possible to understand the meaning of unfamiliar words or phrases.

How does it work? Have the students in a position so that they may make eye contact with each other. The student who is to speak first looks at the line and reads it silently and then looks at the addressee and *says* as much of the line as can be remembered. One must make eye contact with one's partner, who is listening. Eye contact means eye contact. It does not mean just looking in the direction of or staring at one's partner. They should look at each other as if they were actually carrying on a natural, original conversation. One may look back at one's lines as often as necessary, but whenever speaking *must make eye contact*. Generally, I find that most beginning students remember about three words before looking back at the script. Gradually, however, the student will begin to say the words in sense groups. When the student has finished speaking, the respective partners look at their lines and follow the same procedure.

The talk-and-listen system may seem very similar to Michael West's "Read and Look Up" technique. In fact I feel that perhaps it too was founded through a drama experience. There are a couple of additions, not differences, between it and talk-and-listen. First, always *talk* to someone, and second *listen* to the response.

Mr. West states " ... [the student] has to carry the words of a whole phrase, or perhaps a whole sentence, in his mind. The connection is not from book to mouth, but from book to brain, and then from brain to mouth. That interval of memory constitutes half the learning process." (Michael West, *Teaching English in Difficult Circumstances* (London: Longmans, 1961), p. 12.)

Talk-and-Listen Cards

A simple device to train students in the talk-and-listen system is the use of talk-and-listen cards. The cards contain a short scene of usually not more than ten lines between two people. Prepare cards that are suitable for your students. They may be made taken from a play script, dialogues from the textbook, or, better still, write your own. Each card will have the lines of only one speaker; therefore, it becomes necessary for the student to listen to understand the content of the scene. Because the scenes are short, the one will realize that one can remember the lines using the talk-and-listen system. Also, it is easier for you to be sure that everyone is following the rules of talk-and-listen.

Let's use the following dialogue as an example.
A: When can I see you again?
B: It's up to you. You're the boss.
A: How about the day after tomorrow?
B: Sure. What are your plans?
A: I'd rather not say.
B: Oh, you're full of surprises, aren't you?

Put all of A's dialogue on one card, and all of B's on a second, like this:
A: When can I see you again?
B: ....
A: How about the day after tomorrow?
B: ....
A: I'd rather not say.
B: ....

B's card would start like this.
A: ....
B: It's up to you. You're the boss.
A: ....
(etc.)

You may discover that some students have a tendency not to listen to their partners. In such a case prepare another set of cards with two dialogues on each card as follows:

Card A
1. It was good to see you yesterday.
   or
   Did you know I was going to Detroit?
2. Yeah, I'm going to Detroit.
   or
   It was a good party wasn't it?
3. Permanently, I'm moving there.
   or
   Are you going to the picnic Saturday?
4. Depends? On what?
   or
   No, I'll miss this place.

Card B
1. No, I didn't.
   or
   It was good to see you too.
2. Yeah, it was okay.
   or
   For how long?
3. Oh, not on a vacation then?
   or
   I'm not sure, it depends.
4. We'll miss you too.
   or
   Oh. Just depends.

Once you are sure students are listening you may return to the regular talk-and-listen cards.

First have the students read the lines to themselves silently, then using the talk-and-listen method have them *say* the lines. Students may refer to their cards as often as necessary, *but* whenever they are speaking they must make eye contact with their partners.

After the students understand and can use the talk-and-listen system, you are ready to begin utilizing the variety of uses to be made of these handy cards.

Very often students of a new language get into the habit of talking in a monotone, forgetting to make use of the great variety of intonations that they use in their own language to make that language more expressive. To help them make use of these (intonations) tones, have the students use the cards in the following way—always, of course, in a natural voice without strain:

1. Use their highest possible voices.
2. Use their lowest possible voices.
3. One uses the high tone, the other low.

If your students have difficulty arriving at a low or high voice, have them say the first word on their card. Then note by note have them go up or down as far as they can without strain until you reach the desired tone.

Have the students go through another run through of the cards in natural voice or high/low voices doing these things:

1. Speak as rapidly (but clearly) as possible.
2. Speak as slowly as possible.
3. One speaks rapidly, the other slowly.

You and your students will be amazed at how these simple additions will change feeling, meaning and/or the character of the lines.

This is not all that can be done with the cards. We are now ready to add the real acting. How would the students say these lines if:

1. A and B are lovers.
2. A and B have just robbed a bank.
3. A is a dentist, B a patient.
4. A loves B, but B does not love A.
5. A or B is a vistor from another city.

You can think of many other situations.

To make it even more interesting discuss then add other things to develop the situations more fully.

Where does the scene take place?
What were they doing before the dialogue started?
What time is it?
What is the weather like?

All of these things will affect the way the lines are spoken. We certainly use a different tone when talking in church than we do at the ball park, and a hot humid day gives us a completely different feeling from a bitter cold day.

"Each actor has his own special attributes. ... They spring from varied sources. ... Each change of circumstances, setting, place of action, time—brings a corresponding adjustment.

All types of communication ... require adjustments peculiar to each."

Constantin Stanislavski
An Actor's Handbook

After you have worked on the scenes in many different ways you might want to go one step further by asking what happens, after the dialogue, on the card, and continue the scene. What do they say or do?

Other talk-and-listen cards may be made from the following dialogues:

A: Where are you going?
B: I'm going to the store.
A: May I go with you?
B: Yes, but I'm coming right back.
A: I'm tired of sitting with nothing to do.
B: Nothing to do?

A: Have you been to the circus?
B: No. Where is it?
A: It's playing at the arena.
B: How long will it be there?
A: About two weeks, I think.
B: Perhaps I can go next week.

A: Why must you go?
B: I've explained it so many times.
A: Don't you think I care what happens to you?
B: Yes, I'm sure you do.
A: I want you to stay.
B: You're like a phonograph.

A: Do you want these books?
B: Yes, I do.

22

A: Then would you please put them over here.
B: Oh, I'm sorry, I didn't realize they were in the way.
A: I think I've told you that before.
B: Maybe, but I don't remember.

A: This is a beautiful day.
B: I knew it would be like this.
A: Should we start?
B: Yes, why not?
A: Where's the food?
B: Oh, my, that fixes everything.
A: What do you mean?
B: I left it on the bus.

A: May I trouble you?
B: It seems you have.
A: Oh, sorry.
B: Well?
A: I need some help.
B: Help?
A: Yes, in finishing this.
B: By when?
A: Tonight. Could you give me a hand?
B: Sure.
A: Oh, thanks.
B: For what? I said I could, I didn't say I would.

A: Where is my suitcase?
B: It will be here soon.
A: But I was the first off the plane.
B: I know, but it can't be helped.
A: I want to get home and change, I'm soaking wet.
B: So am I, it's so humid.

A: Did you call?
B: No, I didn't.
A: That's funny, I was sure you did.
B: No, I was just sitting here ... thinking.
A: Thinking? About what?
B: The past ... the future ... you know it's strange.

Using talk-and-listen cards is a big change from the regular English lesson, and you will probably find that your students will laugh a great deal and enjoy using them. When students are relaxed and enjoying themselves their minds and bodies are capable of learning.

ACT I

Quite naturally I hope you are using this book to produce a play in English. If, however, you find that you are limited by time or conditions there are numerous activities connected with drama training that you will find useful in the language classroom. In addition to the exercises in this section, you might find that the topics of "Physicalization," "Activities," and "Sense Memory," discussed in Act II will also be helpful classroom activities.

IMPROVISATION

Through spontaneity we are re-formed into ourselves . . . . Spontaneity is the moment of personal freedom when we are faced with reality and see it, explore it and act accordingly. In this reality the bits and pieces of ourselves function as an organic whole.

Viola Spolin
Improvisation for the Theater

It can develop a greater command of the language (oral and written).

Peter Chilver
Improvised Drama

Improvisation is one of the oldest forms of theatre; the most famous example being the Italian Commedia dell'Arte. Today, too, there are many groups which give improvisation performances. The only difference between your improvisations and those for entertainment is that the latter are performed for an audience. In the theatre, improvisation may be used for any number of reasons: to work on relationships between actors, to discover one's real behavior in a given situation, to rekindle spontaneity, to create environment, etc. For language students, it is a chance to use the English each knows, to test, in a relaxed manner, their own ability to cope with various situations, and to learn to think on their feet. The students should follow all the hints for good acting while performing an improvisation as they would if they were performing in a play. That is, they should remain relaxed, keep their concentration, develop their actions or aims, and perform the necessary activities.

The early improvisations of your students should be simple ones that are easily within their reach. I have found it helpful to start with a radio or T.V. interview-type improvisation. This gives students a chance to be up front, but allows them to be seated and, therefore, a little more secure. Unless you have a very advanced student in the group, the teacher/director should be the interviewer.

In all improvisations use props whenever possible because it will help the students in their concentration and, thus, reduce nervousness. For the interview improvisation you will need a microphone. My "microphone" has usually been my fountain pen or a flashlight, but any number of things could be substituted as well. Of course, so many students have cassette recorders now that a real microphone is no problem. Also, you may wish to record the entire proceedings to listen to later. You will need to judge if your students are ready to listen to themselves. Hearing one's own voice can be quite a shock the first time, especially when speaking a foreign language.

The first time you do the interview improvisation, the students should be themselves, and the interviewer should ask about three questions to each student. At another time, let them plan on being someone else, a famous person, real or imaginary—this will give them a chance to use their imaginations.

A second step in improvisation is to get them on their feet. This time for their own security let them work in a small group with no specific roles. They will each be themselves again. A situation that often helps bring about group unity is the stuck elevator. Arrange a small space in the corner of the room the size of a small elevator. You may use chairs to outline the space for the elevator. Have five or six students get in "the elevator" and discuss whatever they might be talking about after class. On a given signal (bell, clapping hands, etc.) from the teacher/director, the "elevator" stops between floors. There is no phone or alarm bell in this elevator. What do the students do? How do they get out?

The students should be advised beforehand that they should try and imagine what they would really do in the situation. In Japan I used this improvisation and the students did nothing, they stood and waited. I asked after the improvisation why they hadn't yelled or banged on the walls. They all assured me that in time someone would realize the elevator was stuck and get them out. "Old Japan hands" informed me that this was probably honest behavior. I was all ready to accept this cultural difference when three of these students the next week were trapped between floors in the school elevator. The banging and yelling could be heard throughout the building. I point this out not only as an amusing anecdote, but also to note that one does not always know how one behaves in a situation until one is actually confronted with it.

The next type of improvisation I use is a group effort involving some movement. These might include situations in a coffee house, on a picnic or a sightseeing tour. Have the students start the improvisation as soon as they are in the acting area. Thus, in the coffee house the improvisation would start as they entered, not after they were seated.

Once the students are adjusted to these simple improvisations, advance to the most useful type of improvisation. These are improvisations with conflict.

An important factor in an improvisation is conflict. This helps the students by giving them a direction and goal for their conversation. Generally, we do not know what people will say to us or what the thoughts behind their words are. This should be true in an improvisation, too. Therefore, it is a good idea to give the information of the goal of each participant privately. I usually give the "who, what, where, and when" of each situation to everyone, and then give cards with more specific information or goals to each participant.

Example:

General Information: Two students share a room in a dormitory or rooming house. It is 10:30 P.M. Student A is trying to sleep. Student B is typing a paper.

Card A: You have been working at a part-time job and are tired. You have a test tomorrow, and will get up at 5 A.M. to study.

Card B: Your paper must be handed in tomorrow morning. You are a "night person" and find it difficult to get up early.

Since all improvisations are open ended, the students may not be able to solve the situation, and the teacher/director will have to stop the improvisation after three to five minutes. If student A and B should resolve the problem, then, of course, the improvisation is over.

Some teachers fear that it is unfair to have two or three students performing in an improvisation in which the rest of the class is not participating. I firmly believe that the rest of the class is not just sitting idly by, but is participating at a much higher level than in most language classrooms. First, they are hearing a new voice using English; they know the teacher/director can speak English, but are curious about their peers' ability. More important than this, however, is that I have found students so involved with the situation that they will audibly advise their fellow students. This proves that they are thinking in English, "Why doesn't he say . . .," or "I would say or do . . . ."

As further proof of this, and to get more mileage out of your improvisation, have one or two other groups perform the same improvisation. You will see marked improvement. Of course, these students have had the security of their desks to plan some of their dialogue and action, but they do not know what their partners have planned, so the improvisation is still valid.

At the early stages of improvisation, students will likely tend to be performing for the audience rather than "living the scene." More than likely, too, most of the situation will turn out to be humorous, for the student feels secure when he hears the laughter of his classmates. Since I am a great believer in the happy, relaxed classroom, I permit this. Later as the students are more relaxed and sure of themselves, I urge them to keep within the framework of the situation. That is, to use the other actors and to behave as they honestly feel they would in the given situation.

Some improvisations to try:

Group:

1. A group of students are at a coffee shop, soda fountain, or lunch room. What do they order and what do they talk about? Suppose one forgot his wallet. How does the waiter or waitress behave?

2. A group of tourists are at an attraction near your area. One student can be the guide to answer questions. How do tourists behave? What are their activities?

3. Students are planning an outing. When will they go? What will they take? How long will they stay? Where will they go? Do all students agree on all arrangements?

4. A group of people are at the veterinarian's office. What kind of animal does each have? What do the people talk about?

Scenes with conflicts:

1. A and B are strangers and are walking in opposite directions. They both see a half dollar on the sidewalk. What do they do? Suppose they are friends walking together?

2. A needs to borrow some money from B. Why does A need the money? B does not want to let A have the money, for often A is careless with money and also A owes B some money that A borrowed a month ago.

3. A loaned a textbook to B. The examination is in two days and A needs the book to study. B has lost the book somewhere, and the bookstore is out of the book, so B cannot buy a replacement.

4. A invites B to dinner. B thinks A is very wealthy and suggests an expensive restaurant. Actually A makes a good impression, but usually has very little money. They go to the expensive restaurant, but A has only about half the money to pay the bill.

I asked a class of young businessmen to bring in situations in which they had used English. This provided excellent improvisations for the other members of the class, and a chance for them to review their handling of the situation. Perhaps you can have your students do the same, or have them provide you with possible situations where they could use English.

All of these situations will be greatly influenced by location and all surrounding circumstances. Take, for example, the group planning the outing. Where is the discussion taking place—the school cafeteria or the library?, a dormitory room or a classroom? Also, is it winter or summer?, raining or clear?, early in the morning or late at night? Everything will affect the way things are said.

Students often want to know how to start thinking in English, here is an acting exercise to help them. It is called "dubbing," which means one set of students does the moving (acting) and another set does the speaking (dubbing). First have a simple meeting of two people. The "actors" must *listen* to the dubbers and move accordingly, likewise the dubbers must be aware of any move made by the actors that would call for specific language. Then, reverse roles.

After you have tried this a few times enlarge your group and give them a more specific situation. Planning a party, shopping, dining in a restaurant, almost any situation will work well. You will notice that the "actors" very often try to coax particular ideas from their dubbers, thus they are thinking in English.

BEING ONESELF OR ROLE PLAYING

"Closeness to your part we call perception of yourself in the part and the part in you ... you can speak for your character in your own person.... Bring yourself to the point of taking hold of a new role concretely, as if it were your own life.

"Do you expect an actor to invent all sorts of new sensations, or even a new soul, for every part he plays? Can he tear out his own soul and replace it by one he has rented as being more suitable to a certain part? You can borrow "things" of all sorts, but you cannot take feelings from another person. My feelings are inalienably mine, and yours belong to you in the same way. You can understand a part, sympathize with the person portrayed, and put yourself in his play, so that you will act as he would. That will arouse feelings in the actor that are analogous to those required for the part. Those feelings will belong not to the person created by the author of the play, but to the actor himself.

"It is extremely important to an actor's creative state to feel what we call "I am." I exist here and now as part of the life of a play, on the stage.... To help an actor find himself in his role and the role in himself ... let him decide sincerely how to answer the question: What would I do here and now, if in real life I had to act under circumstances analogous to those in which my part is set?

"Therefore, no matter how much you act, how many parts you take,

28

you should never allow yourself any exception to the role of using your own feelings.

"Always act in your own person. ... You can never get away from yourself. The moment you lose yourself on the stage marks the departure from truly living your part and the beginning of exaggerated, false acting."

Constantin Stanislavski
An Actor's Handbook

There is likely to be some misunderstanding of the term "role playing" between those teaching a foreign language and actors. Most of the more recent and up-to-date books on acting avoid the term completely. In the theater we do not approve of "role-playing" actors, as it has connotations of stock actors with their bag of tricks which they pull out to fit various play situations. Viola Spolin in *Improvisations for the Theater*, defines role playing as follows: "Role-Playing: as opposed to playing a role; imposing a character as opposed to creating a role out of the problem; artificial imposition of character on self as opposed to allowing natural growth to evolve out of relationship; using a character to hide behind; a mask keeping one from exposure; withdrawal; solo performance."

We must help students to grow and be themselves, able to function with another language and culture with true communication.

To be a good actor we need to understand ourselves and the way we relate to others. We must be aware of our motivations, our activities, and our actions in dealing with others and *ourselves*. We need to learn how we feel and behave in daily life and then transfer these feelings and actions to the stage.

Many teachers of foreign languages (usually the native speakers) give their pupils names taken from the language being studied. The student then pretends to be Joe or Mike. Everyone usually thinks this is a wonderful idea and feels this is a toe in the hot water of culture and language learning. I can think of only two values in such a practice. First, the students do learn a lot of foreign names, and discover which are male and female (often a tremendous problem), and, second, it saves foreign teachers from their own culture/language learning by not having to learn the seemingly difficult names of their students.

Learn your students real names! They will be pleased with the fact that you know who they are. They will know they have made an impression on you with their true identity. With this kind of security, they are better equipped to accomplish their and your goals.

From an acting point of view, I believe that no one can be other than himself. Alice cannot be Chieko or Satoshi, Bill. Good actors do not put

on the "coat of the character" showing us all of the external characteriza-
tions of the role they are playing, rather they make the character become
themselves. It may seem like a fine point whether the actor becomes the
character or the character the actor, but it is an important fine point for
the security and development of the foreign language student.

I have been told many times of the success teachers have had with role
playing. Virtually all of these related to very shy students, who when
given a short dialogue and a cape, or a prop, suddenly became "someone
else." In this case the magic of theatre had worked its miracle. The
situation, the costume, or the prop had released a spark within these
students which was a part of them, and had always been present waiting
for release. They had been freed momentarily to express a part of themselves that usually existed in their daydreams or imagination. What often
happens at this point is that students often cling to the feeling of that
moment and with the aid of this "mask" (cape and sword) continues to
"act" that one moment throughout the dialogue. Thus a real moment is
turned into a pretense. The drama method is aimed at helping students
to free themselves to express their true feelings on a moment-to-moment
basis. When students understand that this is a part of themselves, they
have this freedom always.

Relaxation

Perhaps the most important word in the learning process, and certainly
vital in creative activities is relaxation. It was a big surprise for me to
learn that often students taking the same course did not know each other.
This was true in Japan and the United States. It is impossible to create,
or to be really relaxed with strangers about. Therefore, on the first day of
class the first order of business is self-introductions. Ask the students to
remember the names of all the people in the class. The students should
keep the introductions simple—"My name is _____ ." The second
day ask the students to introduce the person on right or their left and
the following day the person sitting across from them. Keep this up until
you are sure that everyone knows everyone else by name. And be sure
you know all the names, too. To add to the fun of this—oh, it will be fun
and cause a great deal of laughter at the struggle to remember everyone's
name—one day as each person is introduced, have them say something
special about themselves that makes them different. What type of music
do they like? What is their favorite color, food, movie ... anything?
Often people will remember the special "secret" before they remember
the name.

Another way of having them learn names, and a bit of cultural behavior, is to have an imaginary party. Decide on several suitable "drinks" to be served and tell them to your group. You, as host, take the "tray" to each of the students and have them ask for and take their "drinks." The students should continue to "hold" and "use" the "glass" throughout the party. Show them a simple informal introduction by Student A and B and introducing them to one another.

"José, this is Maria. Maria, José." Student A (José) then introduces Maria to Student C. B next introduces C to D and so on until each student has performed an introduction.

The "party" is good because it gets students up, forcing them to think on their feet without the security of the desk or table. By concentrating on "holding" or "using" their drinks self-consciousness and nervousness are minimized.

This is the first step toward relaxation. The breathing and voice exercises described earlier will also help. You will need to watch for little signs of tension and nervousness in your students, for not only are they not relaxed when they display these signs, but also they are wasting energy which should be used elsewhere. It is impossible to list all the tell-tale signs of tension but some of the most common are clenched fists, rigid thumbs (or other fingers), a wiggly knee, a tapping foot, swinging leg, or a foot turned on its side. Subconsciously these tense spots are where the concentration is and is also where the audience will focus its attention if it should happen on stage.

To remove these tensions stand up and shake. Holding the hands out, shake violently. The same may be done with the feet—one at a time of course. An exercise that my students enjoyed for relaxation and that also helped them be more aware of their bodies was the big shake. Start by moving one finger, now five fingers, now ten. Add each movement one at a time—the wrist, the elbows, the shoulders, the head, one foot, the knee, one hip, both hips. It is not so easy, but I guarantee your class will be relaxed and there will be laughter.

Tenseness is also likely to concentrate in the neck. To relax roll the head back, then to the right, then forward letting it drop naturally and last bring it up left and back. Repeat this several times, and then reverse the movement.

This is another excellent relaxing exercise. Be sure the feet are flat on the floor spread slightly apart. With the arms over the head reach for the ceiling. Stretch and stretch and try to touch the ceiling. Now quickly bend over and shake your arms, head and body. A variation on this is that once you are stretching to tighten the muscles in order—arms, body, buttocks, thighs, and calves. Then shake out.

31

When you feel your class is ready for it, let them be animals or birds. Move about the room and make the sound of an animal. I generally start off by asking the boys to be ducks and the girls to be big birds flying about the room. Try to get full sounds and movements. Don't forget *you* may have to do this, too, to get them started.

A quick relaxing exercise that is useful just before entering the stage, making a speech, or when you feel yourself getting tense in a situation and you cannot be physical, is to take a very deep breath then exhale it completely.

Concentration

Creativeness is, first of all, the complete concentration of the entire nature of the actor.

An actor must have a point of attention, and this must not be in the auditorium. In real life there are always . . . objects that fit our attention, but conditions in the theater are different, and interfere with an actor's living normally, so that *an effort* to fix attention becomes necessary . . . to learn to look at things, on the stage, *and to see them.*

Constantin Stanislavski
An Actor's Handbook

Concentration is necessary to succeed as an actor or as a student. Very early in life we have excellent concentration, but as we get older we often lose our ability. Through drama it is possible to help students regain this ability which will help them overcome their insecurities and self-consciousness. You will note that many of the exercises later in this book will be exercises greatly involved with concentration.

Often when we ask our students to concentrate, we get a bunch of blank faces staring ahead at nothing, or at the object being demonstrated or exhibited. It is necessary, therefore, to help students develop their concentration to get them away from this erroneous habit. Concentration is the ability to focus one's attention (all of his senses) on a particular object or area. One must be able to shift one's concentration where it is needed in order to focus the audience's attention where one wishes.

In order that the audience's attention is kept on the play, actors must keep their concentration on the stage. An actor who is concerned with (concentrating on) the audience is not a good actor and is likely to have stage fright. Remember, discussing concentration with your students is language learning.

Some exercises to help develop concentration follow, and you will be able to adapt them and create others. Let's start off with some simple exercises.

1. What sounds do you hear? Have your students close their eyes and listen to sounds. Do not make sounds but have them call out (or write) the sounds they hear. With a little experimentation you will be amazed at how many sounds are present around us all of the time, yet we are able to shut out most of them when we need to. Their list of sounds (which is also an aid in building vocabulary) might include breathing, coughing, footsteps, a buzzing fly, a telephone ring, a pencil sharpener, a car horn, car brakes, talking, laughing, a flushing toilet, a bird, a door closing, an airplane, a key in a lock, a radio, and insects. The list may go on and on. I made this list while sitting in my office listening.

2. What colors do you see in the room?

3. What things do you see? (This may get to be too large a list, so you might want to only use the objects on one desk or a wall.)

4. What textures are there in the room? Or what do things feel like?

5. What smells can you smell?

We can now jump to a memory list.

1. Imagine the tastes of various foods. (Students should name the foods.)

2. What sounds do you hear at a circus?

3. What is in your handbag? Briefcase? Pockets? (No looking—try to remember.)

4. What clothes did you have on yesterday?

5. What are the smells in a department store or market place?

Next get up and move and use our bodies (also good for relaxation).

1. Move like some animal. Try to capture the attitudes that the animal has.

2. Next add the animal's sound as you move.

3. Imagine about two feet of space all around you. Move about the room without letting anyone into your circle of space. It's not as easy as it seems in an average-sized room.

4. Create an emotion (happy, angry, nervous, etc.) as you move about.

5. What other words express those same emotions? Collect three or four from the students (help them if they need it). Move about the room repeating these words in a given order and in the proper attitude. Example: "Happy, laughing, joyous, delightful," etc.

You probably have discovered that your students are relaxed and not self-conscious about speaking a few words in a new language, in a loud voice, and in front of others. Most of the words have come from them, they have learned the feeling behind some of the words, and have used the words immediately.

Let's narrow our concentration now to increase the focus.

1. Hold up an object and have your students tell you as much about it as they can.

For example, hold a flashlight up. It might elicit the following responses.

It is an instrument to give light.
It makes a spot of light.
The spot can be made larger or smaller.
It is mostly silver metal.
It has glass at one end.
There is a mirror cone under the glass.
There is a light bulb in the middle of the cone.
There is a ring at the other end.
It has a black plastic button that pushes up to turn the light on.
Both ends will screw off.
There is a spring inside the end that has a ring on it.
There are two batteries inside.
The batteries give the power.
The batteries are covered with metal.
The metal is printed in blue and red with black lettering.

2. Now, have a student explain another object to a friend in the class. Careful about corrections! Don't be too eager to correct them, but help them over the rough spots.

3. Have two students perform an improvisation (see section on improvisation). Let one explain an object while the other asks questions about it.

4. Have the class make up a story about the object. Of course, this is the imaginary history of the object. You might want to start them off if there is hesitation, but be sure they keep to the subject.

Example: This flashlight is very old (it doesn't matter if it's brand new). It was found about three years ago outside a cave. Three boys, during their summer vacation about seven years ago, went camping. They have never returned. The flashlight was discovered three years ago and it was identified by one of the boys' parents. You can see the initials scratched here on the side. Everyone assumed the boys were lost in the cave, but no trace of them was found inside. The family keeps this flashlight as a source of hope that the boys will return.

ACT I

Imagination

You can kill the King without a sword and you can light a fire without matches. What needs to burn is your imagination.

Constantin Stanislavski
An Actor's Handbook

The stage is not real yet actors must make it seem real to the audience and to themselves. Everything they do on stage should be the result of their imagination. All of the exercises in this book should require your students to use their imaginations. You will need to guide your students to hunt for all the possibilities in portraying a character rather than resorting to the obvious or to a cliché. Thieves do not necessarily sneak around a room and slip things carefully in their pocket. They may, very openly, pick it up and walk out with the object in their hands.

Bring in objects, common everyday items, and see how many ways your students can think of to use them. For example, a cardboard shoe box may be used as a filing box, a television or still camera, a piece of modern art, a jewel box, or a trash box. Have your students show you what it is rather than tell you.

With these same props have your students develop improvisations or stories using the same prop as various objects. With exotic props or costumes, have your students do improvisations. Start a story then call on one of your students to continue the story. Allow each student to contribute a few lines.

Observation

An actor should be observant not only on stage but also in real life. He should concentrate with all his being on whatever attracts his attention .... There are people gifted by nature with powers of observation .... When you hear such people talk you are struck by the amount that an unobservant person misses.

Constantin Stanislavski
An Actor's Handbook

Observation is so closely related to concentration that it may seem unnecessary to have a special section about it. However, since all of the acting exercises are so closely interrelated I feel that it will be valuable for your students to have this special section.

An actor needs to be aware of the way he handles or looks at objects. As we move about our homes we may pay little attention to the things

35

around us. Yet, in a moment of embarrassment or deep thought we may look very carefully at the glass we are holding, peer down at the ice and study its slightest movement, rub the moisture off the side of the glass and observe every detail of the glass and its contents as if it were a rare object. These differences in the acuteness of observation will have an affect on the way you speak.

It is also helpful to the actor to observe people and their behavior. By using their imagination the student can decide who the person is, what job they have, where they live, are they married or single, what sports they participate in, and any number of such things. If the student sees a person who seems to fit the characters they are portraying they may then study the physical actions plus using their imagination to find useful information to adapt for the stage.

In most parts of the world now students have many opportunities to observe English-speaking people. An enterprising English-Speaking Society in Kamakura, Japan, offered free guide service for a walking tour of their city. They set up a large sign at the railroad and bus station to attract the visitors who were not on a guided tour. This meant that usually one student ended up accompanying two tourists. This is an excellent opportunity for students to practice their English, observe behavior, and to be of service. If there are no tourists or businessmen about, they may observe films and television shows concentrating on the behavioral aspects as well as the story.

There are numerous exercises which may be used to help develop observational powers. Perhaps start off by having your students observe all of their movements while doing an everyday task.

At home they may observe such things as how they brush their teeth, shave, eat, or tie their shoelaces. In the classroom they might study how they sharpen a pencil, take notes, look up a word in a dictionary, and so forth.

To see how well they observed these things have them perform the task without using the props. Make sure that their movements are as accurate as possible and not mere indication. The students should also perform these tasks giving the unseen objects the proper weight and shape. Let me warn you that the activities they choose should be simple ones or part of a more complete activity. Often I have seen beginning actors "prepare a meal" as an exercise.

Naturally, it was mostly indication, because to do it well would take a year of concentrated study.

Another exercise would be to have the students describe to the class in greatest possible detail a person or event that they had observed the day before.

In addition, you could ask them to observe someone doing a job and then to perform "that job" before the other students. Here again you should watch that they do the detailed movements naturally rather than merely indicate.

You could also show them a famous painting and then have them assume the poses of the people in the painting. To carry this two steps further, have them bring "the painting" to life. How do the people move? What are they saying?

SCENE STUDY

Most acting students spend a great deal of time on scene study. You may find it a valuable asset also.

The scenes that are used are usually short (about two pages) and contain something of special interest for the acting student—an acting problem or objective, a dramatic moment, or even a chance to make a scene truthful. Generally, the scenes should involve only two people in order that the students may work on them easily without having to schedule an entire cast.

In nearly every case the entire play should be read in order to see exactly how the scene fits into the play, and for the student to fully understand the characters. Work on scenes should be approached in exactly the same way as work on a play.

Suitable scenes may be taken from any play that fits your need. Also, there are books of collected scenes available. I have listed one such book below, as well as some plays which need only two performers.

50 Great Scenes for Student Actors—edited by Levy Olfson
> Bantam Book Inc., Dept. WD, Room 2450, 666 5th Avenue, New York, NY 10019

The Fourposter—1 man, 1 woman
> Follows a marriage from wedding day until the couple packs up and moves out of their home thirty-five years later.
> S.F., $1.50

Lovers and Other Strangers—See page 169.

One Day In the Life of Ivy Dennison—See page 159.

Owl and the Pussycat—Bill Manhoff—1 man, 1 woman
> Concerns a stuffy young author and a prostitute he has been spying on.
> S.F., $1.50

ACT I

Two For the Seesaw—William Gibson—1 man, 1 woman
> A young dancer who seems doomed to always make others happy
> becomes involved with a lonesome lawyer who has left his wife
> and come to New York to "find himself."
> S.F., $1.50

38

ACT II

I cannot overemphasize the satisfaction that you and your students will receive from performing a play. If you have tried some of the activities suggested in Act I then I urge you to try a play. Most of the activities in this book are those that are being used to train actors today for the professional stage in the United States. All of the activities have proven to be helpful to student "actors" learning English.

When I suggest that you perform a play I mean a classroom performance. All of the information included in Acts I and II are suitable for the classroom. Act III is concerned with the physical production if you decide to put your play on the stage.

Once again let me remind you that everyone can act. Our daily lives are made up of a series of performances adapted to fit the various situations and audiences that we encounter. From earliest childhood we learned, or were taught, how to act. Crying babies can compel their parents to feed them, pick them up, or change them. Their objective is to get one of these accomplished; their concentration is to get the parents' attention; and their physical activity is the kicking of feet in the air. As children grow they continue their "lessons," plus they have learned some of the rules of the game. They know exactly how to act (behave) to get the desired results from parents, grandparents, and playmates. Of course, the parents, grandparents, and playmates have learned the rules of the game, too. Conflict! We now have a mini-drama, which reminds us of the old adage, "Life is drama," and equally true, drama is life.

PLAY SELECTION

The first major concern in production certainly would be in selecting a play, and obtaining it. In the Epilogue, I have given a selected list of plays that I feel are suitable for teaching English. I have also included information about where such plays may be obtained and the current prices. Please do not think that this is a complete list of suitable plays.

ACT II

Like a Broadway director, choose a play that interests you and that you would like to do. You are to be the director and guide. If you are not interested in the play, it will be very difficult for you to get the students interested in the project. Possibly, for your first play you will want to play safe and select one that you are sure you understand completely and that you can handle easily. This is fine, but don't hesitate later to choose one that offers many challenges. As you work on the play with your students, you will discover many new and interesting things about the play with your students, or things that you may add to the play. Part of this will come from seeing it come alive in front of you and part from what your students bring to it. An accidental interpretation of a line or action may be just the right touch at that moment. An individual trait may bring new meaning to a situation or characterization.

I had often read that Thornton Wilder's one-act play, *The Long Christmas Dinner*, was one of the most beautiful one-act plays in the English language. I had read it, even seen it once or twice, and thought it interesting, but far from one that deserved the praise it had received. When, however, I started to work on it with a group of Japanese students, I soon discovered the magic of the play. I have since directed it twice and feel that I could easily spend a year on it without getting bored with it. The actors and I were constantly discovering new things about the script, or ways to play various scenes.

Your second consideration, and I hesitate to give you any order of importance, should be the dialogue. Is it natural dialogue? That is, is the dialogue in the play meant to be spoken rather than read? Is it the kind of informal language that they can understand outside the classroom —the type of conversation they would use in everyday life? The vocabulary should be modern, with the contractions, clichés, and repetitions which occur in our daily conversations. Also note if the speeches are of normal length. Often there are long expository speeches that are sure to be memorized and difficult to handle.

The next consideration should be the cultural content of the play. Let me hasten to add that the type of culture I'm talking about is of the little "c" variety. Are the situations of the play those in which students could possibly find themselves? Are the situations those that demonstrate clearly the use of the language?

It may seem unnecessary to add this next item about selecting a play, but I know of too many cases where it was overlooked. That is, can you cast the play? If you have all males in your class it would be foolish to select a play that was predominately female, or vice versa. By the same token, if a *major* character must be tall or short or fat or skinny and you have no one to fit such a role, then select another play. There are a number of suitable plays for all male and female casts, and often small roles may be rewritten to suit your needs. Our imagination will generally take care of extreme age or youth but will fail us if there are too many references to the physical appearances of an individual.

Keeping the preceding points in mind you should then choose a play that (1) will be interesting to you and the students, (2) has modern language, (3) shows today's culture and behavior, and (4) is easy to cast.

On the negative side there are certain plays to beware of, especially since so many well-meaning people are likely to suggest them to you if you let it be known you are doing a play. Oh, how often I've heard, "You teach English through drama, do you? How well I remember when I was studying English. We always presented one of the great Shakespearean plays. I was in *Macbeth*. Such beautiful language. I remember the lines still." The awe and respect that nearly everyone has for Shakespeare causes us to talk in a strange and artificial way. There is no denying that Mr. S. was the greatest playwright in the English language, but I do not feel that his plays are suitable for language learning. Shakespeare is big "C" Culture and students of literature need to know his works, but for someone learning English his plays are not the most useful. The sentence structure, patterns, and a good bit of the vocabulary are those of Elizabethan England and are so far removed from us today that if students were to use them they would certainly sound most strange. Add to this the difficulty of understanding the plays. Since the scholars have disagreed for years on the meaning of various passages, we should not expect a foreign student to fully grasp the meaning.

Frequently, you may see an article in some of the educational journals suggesting the use of scenes from the classics to stimulate interest in English. I am firmly convinced that with the relatively new student it has just the opposite effect. An advanced student of English, who became very interested in drama, asked to borrow some of the great plays. One of the plays I loaned him was the great classic comedy, *The Importance of Being Earnest*. The dialogue is crisp and witty and, I think, a joy to hear and read. When the student returned the book to me, he commented that it was the dullest play he had ever read, and he could see nothing funny in it. The language and the culture were too out-dated for him to understand. In defense of the play, I will add that he was reading it, rather than performing or seeing it. The language, situation, and culture of most of the classic plays usually do not fit the language students need.

Another type of play to avoid (and this could include some very good plays) are the ones which are written in poetic form. A student facing a

41

page of verse is more than likely going to be "turned off" just by the visual image. If they should accept it, they probably will be caught in the trap of the meter or the rhyme.

Along with the good poetic dramas are a large number of bad plays that pretend to be better than they are by using verse. The vocabulary of such plays is often not useful in daily conversation. *Hark*, *ye*, *alas*, *yea*, and *verily* lead us into such lines as:

"Hark, ye mighty gods who dids't kill
the spirit to learn thy English."

Also try to avoid what I choose call the "church basement" type of play, written by untalented nonprofessional writers, who are just like the untalented professional writers. These good people are more concerned with their particular moral and/or ethical message than with anything else, but often the audience never gets the message for they become bored and fall asleep. I hasten to add that this type of play is not confined to the church. In fact today you are more likely to find it used by revolutionaries, politicians, and social reformers anxious to make their views more appealing. It is true that the message is never obscure; therefore, many foreign students are attracted to it, but the dialogue is usually most unnatural and the construction of the play poor.

There are a number of plays that are adaptations of great short stories, usually the ones that are in the public domain. These are generally adapted by scholars and not by playwrights. The dialogue is, therefore, terribly stilted and artificial and again the cultural behavior is difficult even for a native speaker to comprehend. Somewhat in the same line are the famous modern plays and television scripts shortened and adapted for classroom use. Several things happen. By condensing a two-hour play to thirty minutes, things happen too quickly, so that a normal development of conversation and action does not take place. Secondly, a narrator is added who often has considerably more to say than anyone else. Usually what is narrated are the exciting things that happen, leaving the actor with the dull in-between conversations. Choose a play where the action takes place on stage, where the actor gets up and moves so that the play becomes a conversation, not a reading.

Often I have been asked about using plays from the students' own culture that have been translated into English. Many reasons are given for using such plays—the plays are more readily available, the students can translate the plays themselves, they will understand the play and cultural aspects better and, therefore, concentrate on English and do a better job, and the physical production is easier. Even with all of these plus factors I feel that it is not a good idea to use such plays.

ACT II

We must not confuse the students by teaching them English to fit behavioral patterns that would be out of place in English-speaking cultures. The language should fit the situation, so the two may be learned together and be of use to the students when confronted with a real situation. For example, in a Japanese home a guest enters the room and almost immediately sits on the floor. They are served very hot tea which they drink making noise as they draw in a lot of air to keep from burning the mouth. This sound is not heard by the Japanese, but is noticed by all newly arrived Westerners. Students who use this type of behavior fitting it into English, will be in for some rather rude looks when they venture out of their culture. We must teach them daily behavior which goes along with the language.

In a somewhat similar vein if the translation is too literal it does not use the appropriate everyday English for the situation. For example, in Japan it is appropriate for the hostess to say to her guests, "This is miserable food, but if it tastes all right to you, please eat as much as you want." You then see the "miserable" food and realize that hours of labor and a whole month's wages have been spent on the delicious feast. A similar comment could be made in an American home, but it would only be said as a joke.

Another reason for not using translated plays is that the styles of acting may vary a great deal. This is especially true between East and West. The student must necessarily carry over certain qualities that are expected in one's native drama. These qualities vary a great deal, but include such things as special voice placement, special language, movement, and basic acting techniques.

To close the section with a positive note, let me remind you that there are many fine and suitable plays available. For a start I included seven plays in the Epilogue that are simple and easy to perform in the classroom. In addition there is a list of both short and long plays that should be useful for future productions.

IN THE BEGINNING—

Let the students have the play far enough in advance so that they have time to read the play, and to look up words with which they are not familiar. Do not tell the students at this time which role they will be playing. There are several reasons for this. *First,* all their concentration is likely to be on the one role, thus, they would fail to look at the overall picture.

Actors are in the habit of putting their attention only to the roles assigned to them .... This is a mistake .... It is very important that they sense the production as a whole, its entire intent .... Then by itself, the part given to you will become clear.

Constantin Stanislavski
An Actor's Handbook

Second, after a few days of working on a play the teacher/director may wish to change the original casting plan (until I learned this I was often sorry I could not recast). *Third,* the students may start memorizing the lines before they understand or realize that this is *not* what you want them to do. Disappointment or fear of the role assigned is also minimized as the student becomes interested and involved in the whole project, rather than one role or part of the project.

After all of the students are seated in a way that they can easily communicate with each other and you, start your discussion of the play. You may want to tell the story of the play, thus, avoiding making it a "test" of the students understanding by asking *them* to tell the story. Also, you will avoid the possibility of a wrong story line being introduced, which might possibly cause confusion. The story should be told briefly in simple words. Such as: "This play is about a girl who lives in a small town and is planning to marry a local young man. Another young man comes to this town and the girl falls in love with him. Her mother objects to this rough newcomer, but the girl finds him exciting even though he is in trouble with the police. He is forced to leave town and the girl goes with him."

The story of the play should never be hidden or overshadowed by theme or production. It is the roadmap guiding the entire project.

Many students will want to get overly involved with theme. This too should be kept simple so that it can be dealt with. Often a highly dramatic moment may be misunderstood as theme rather than climax. This happened once in Japan with a group that was performing Arthur Miller's *A View from the Bridge,* a powerful play on the destructiveness of jealousy. The students had picked up a dramatic scene near the end of the play when the immigration officers come in to find the illegal entrants as the "theme scene"—the harshness of U.S. immigration to foreigners. Had they stuck to this, they would have destroyed the play.

You might ask if there are words they did not understand, or other questions concerning the play. Most detailed discussion should come when you reach the problem sections of the play. Watch your students carefully while they are rehearsing and if you feel they are not understanding a situation, explain it.

Assign roles for "today only" (or even part of the rehearsal) and begin by using the "talk-and-listen" system.

44

ACT II

When working on a play "talk and listen" will seem slow. You and your students will be tempted to abandon it, and start memorizing to satisfy their and your feeling for progress. Don't! This slow start will give your students a much stronger foundation and all future work will advance more rapidly.

Students should not try to memorize the lines when they are reading it to themselves, but just read it for understanding and then say as much as they can. Don't let the students who feel they are taking too much time abandon "talk and listen." Also watch for those who want to appear advanced and read the lines with quick glances at their partners. Stop them, and keep them on "talk and listen." Do not fear that the students will learn the lines in very broken up sections of three words. Gradually, they will join them together. The first couple of times through it may be three words at a time, then four, five, etc. You may find it interesting to see how you and your friends break up your sentences when you are in relaxed conversation. Hide a recorder and record your social conversation and see what happens. We speak *very* differently from the way we read. If your students or anyone were to talk as they read, we would feel it was a very strange language and most unnatural.

I cannot stress too much the importance of listening. Many famous actors attribute a great deal of their success as actors to the fact that they were good listeners. It is impossible to be a good actor without being a good listener. The same is true in conversation. Unless you listen you cannot be a good conversationalist. We must do two things to succeed in either role . . . talk and listen.

Each time a student goes through a "talk-and-listen" rehearsal they are really going through the play twice. They read it once and speak it once. As they join the words together to form the whole sentence and say them as conversation, they are learning them. You will notice that soon the students are not referring to their script as often. Continue the "talk-and-listen" system as long as you are sitting around the table or at sit-down rehearsals.

Some students may want to work faster, and to save time, they will "almost" memorize their lines at home. If this should happen, change their roles, if possible, and explain the value of the "talk-and-listen" system even though you have already done this. Often I would not assign specific roles for several days until they were adjusted to the system.

Each student should be encouraged to read the play at home, but they should read the entire play or an entire section of the play. They will be tempted to read only their own lines, but they must read the entire play to see how their character fits into the whole situation, and to understand why they are saying their lines. One can only get this if one understands the flow of the play. Most of one's learning will take place during the rehearsal period when one is actually involved in interaction with other students. The home reading is for understanding and familiarization.

Because you are using a printed script and your students now feel they are "doing a play," many of the things they have learned may be forgotten and they will begin to "act." Stop them. This first reading (and several more) is for understanding—to understand the play, the characters, their relationship to each other, the atmosphere of the location and the period. It will be slow going and you may find that you will not progress as far as you had planned. Do not worry about this—you are building a strong foundation. On subsequent meetings discuss what had happened up to the cut off point, and then start a page or so back to get into the scene again. If there are actual scene breaks or obvious sections to start from, then start from any of those.

It is natural that the students will want to begin acting. They can see the emotion that should be taking place, they have ideas about the behavior of the various ages represented and will want to add these things.

This is a tricky time for the teacher/director. The student is likely to start indicating rather than "being" and "doing." We do not want them to get in the habit of surface acting, yet we don't want to thwart those that may be ready to "take off." Usually I try to keep them concentrating on understanding the play itself for the first three rehearsals. After this, if I see that they are honestly relating to each other and listening while sitting around the table, I begin to let them physicalize the character. (Of course, the main aspects of physicalization will take place when you start the blocking rehearsals.) How would the character sit at the table? Would they slouch in their chair or sit up straight? Would everything be neat around them or in disorder? Just how would the character behave given the limitations of being seated at a table? You will notice that there will likely be a change in voice quality and in the rapidity of speaking for we are greatly controlled by our bodily attitudes. Once the students are on their feet and you begin giving them their stage movements they will need to carry their physicalization all the way.

Once you start blocking the movement into the play, the actors will be involved with their activities and stage business. At these times students should make eye contact, when logical, for we do not always look at people when we are talking to them. A mother may only occasionally or never look at her daughter or son while she is sewing or cooking, but conversation does not stop. It may seem foolish to even mention this, but too often amateur actors stop all activity when speaking. Activities will sometimes control the way we speak. The concentration or physical exertion will do many things to our voices.

I do not give a date when I expect the students to work without the scripts. This is a threat and would surely encourage them to memorize. You will be able to tell when the students may possibly be able to work without their books, and at this point just announce that you would like them to try without their scripts. (Do not give even one day's notice.) There will likely be groans and moans from nearly everyone because they feel they are not ready. Insist that they try without the scripts. Some will be surprised at how much they know; others will need help on nearly every line. Let the weak ones have their scripts again. Remind them it's all right to use the script. (I have even said, "You may carry the book during performance if you need to. I want you to communicate rather than recite," however, no one ever carried a script.) You will also note that some students will carry their scripts, but not refer to them. Scripts are their "security blankets." Once they discover that they are not using the script, they will willingly discard them. If you have asked them to work without scripts too soon then everyone has a good laugh about it, and you can continue with the scripts.

Students should read the play at every opportunity to familiarize themselves with it. Stress upon them the importance of reading the entire play or act, rather than just their own scenes or lines.

Actors should never read just their lines or recite them out loud. The lines must always be in response to someone else speaking.

Act I had a brief discussion about the actor always being himself. If you are planning to work on a play, then it needs to be discussed further.

It was stated that the actor does not become the character, but the character becomes the actor.

How does one go about making a character become one with the actor? First, it is important to hunt for the similarities rather than the differences between the character and the actor. We are made up of a number of different traits and facets, and there are sure to be some that apply to both the actor and the character. When actors are given a role they study the character to discover the various qualities of that character. They select those characteristics that they wish to portray, and see if they themselves have those same qualities. Perhaps the character is generally very sad or depressed and the actor asked to play that role is a very happy, easy-going person. Surely this actor must have had some moments when they were depressed. They remember them and the circumstances surrounding them. In a play depicting a rather unpleasant American tourist, an Asian student felt that she had nothing in common with the character. On close examination, one obvious trait of the character was her superiority over the "native peasants." Since the girl playing the role was attending the East-West Center at the University of Hawaii, which is devoted to the understanding of other cultures, she could not admit, even to herself, that

47

she felt superior to anyone else. From an idealistic point of view we do not want to feel superior perhaps, but in actuality we are human beings, and most of us have our prejudices. A four-year-old feels more adult (superior) to the crawling baby. This then is a starting point to build the similarities from.

The actors have their own experiences and feelings to draw from. In addition, they are given the script to study the character and form their interpretation from their own experience and knowledge. To this they can add the "magic if" of theater. If *I* were in this situation how would I behave? What would I do? How would I feel? So far so good, but trouble arises when the playwright has written in a bit of action that the actor would not ordinarily do in their own culture in the given situation. What then? Does it destroy the whole theory? No. This is where drama really can teach us culture and its relationship to language. From the script we can tell by the action described how people behave in a given situation. Also, we can learn if such behavior is the approved behavior in that culture.

Take for instance an extreme example of a scene in which a businessman is very angry over something that has happened in his office. The script calls for him to bang his fist on the desk and shout at his secretary and subordinates. In many cultures, however, a businessman would not behave in such a manner although he would be just as angry over the situation. How would the student go about portraying this scene to make it effective and still express himself? Since we all have the same basic emotions, the student should first try to discover how he feels "inside" when he is angry, but not how he expresses such anger. The feeling must come first. From the script he studies the incident that happened before the outburst. What went wrong that triggered the man's anger? How important is it? Why is the man displaying anger; to get results, or is it annoyance with himself? The student should look to himself to see if he has ever had similar outbursts of anger in other situations, though he may not feel he would in the given situation. If so, he can easily adjust his feelings to the new situation. Through rehearsals and the understanding of his own anger, the student may begin to strike the desk lightly at first and gradually builds the scene until he has reached the proper pitch of anger. What the audience sees then is *his* anger rather than an indication of anger. Even though he may not ever be able to strike the desk as violently or shout as loudly as the playwright intended, the idea that the man is angry is clear to all. The student had not "acted" angry, but has been angry. He has put real meaning for himself to the words and the action. Learning language this way gives the students true security, for they understand that they can express themselves in another language. How much better, and really easier it is for them to express themselves rather than to memorize, not only the words, but also how they were spoken by the teacher (or tape). On the stage mechanical performances denote nothing but the ability of the student to memorize. In real life such a recitation is often considered humorous and cute by speakers of the language being learned ("They were so cute when they tried to speak our language"), and certainly denotes a lack of communication.

Most of the plays and scenes that are suitable for the beginning speaker would not contain such a dramatic moment as the one described above. The scenes should deal with the average daily conversations which express much milder demonstrations of our basic emotions or feelings. These, of course, are easier for the students to perform and are much more useful to them later.

Students will often ask you to tell them how to say a line. I made it a general rule never to "read" or "say" a line for a student. This does not mean that I do not help the student with pronunciation and diction. Students may feel more secure if you tell them how to say a line, but real security comes when they discover that they can find the correct way themselves. The only correct way to say a line is how each individual says it for themselves in context. Even the same individual will say the same line slightly differently each time they say it, depending on how they feel at that moment, what was said to them before, and what they expect to happen when they say the line. There is no right way to say an isolated individual line. Take a simple line such as "Would you give it to me?" The stress obviously can fall on any word depending on the situation. What happened before the line was spoken? What happened after? Also, it will change if the person is happy, sad, angry, jealous, old, young, sick, cold, etc. Furthermore, the intonation may change depending on whom the person is speaking to. Each individual has their own way of dealing with all of these factors, and that will enable them to say the line properly. Of course all punctuation should be followed carefully as an added help.

Do not expect that students will arrive at the perfect way of saying the line immediately even though they have an understanding of all the surrounding factors. They will try but miss many times. Do not push them or try to save time by giving them *your* interpretation. Guide them with hints and reminders of the surrounding factors which they need.

Stanislavski gives us excellent advice regarding this, "There is the director of exceptional talent who shows the actors how to play their parts. Having seen the brilliant handling of his part, the actor will wish to play it just as he has seen it demonstrated. He will never be able to get away from the impression he has received, he will be compelled awkwardly to imitate the model .... After such a demonstration an actor is shorn of his freedom and of his own opinion about his role."

Let every actor produce what he can and not chase after what is beyond his creative powers." (*An Actor's Handbook*)

The study and work on one's self then is the most important aspect of becoming a good actor. It is also most helpful in becoming a good speaker of English.

The rest of this section will discuss other aspects of rehearsing a play. In doing this, the acting exercises in Act I will prove useful.

Emotion

You may be surprised to learn that I suggest that you forget about emotion, since we naturally tend to link acting and emotion together. Directors and actors often talk about "putting feeling" into the scene, but it is well to remember that we cannot act an emotion. We must create the emotion by *doing* something. The actor must always be concerned with his action or objective rather than his feeling.

Recently there was an earthquake felt here at the East-West Center. When the jolt came no one acted fear. The first thoughts, which only took a moment, were "What is that?" With the realization that it was an earthquake some people ran out of the building, others rushed to stand in a doorway, the largest number got under the tables. One person in a loud clear voice suggested that everyone protect his head. After it was over people commented on how frightened they had been. The realization of this fear then came after they reviewed the situation.

A moment after the first tremor they were *doing* something—protecting themselves. Had anyone been watching the scene they would have been aware that the people were afraid, through their actions they had created the emotion of fear.

When your students talk about "putting in emotion" remind them to put in the actions, imagination, concentration, and activities instead.

Actions

The action of a character in a play is the objective of that character. The movement on stage (blocking) will be discussed later. Stanislavski said, "Spectators come to the theatre to hear the sub-text. They can read the text at home." If an entire play could be captured on the printed page, then there would be no need for it to be performed. This subtext is what the actors and directors bring to the script to make it come to life, and, therefore, make for the magic of the theatre. Perhaps you have seen a performance of a good script, when the set was excellent. The actors moved about the stage well and recited their lines without making a mistake. Yet the play was unsatisfactory. What had happened was that the actors had failed to provide you with the subtext—they had not supplied the actions necessary to bring the play to life. It would have been better if you had read the play, and with your imagination supplied at least part of the subtext.

In our daily lives almost everything we say has a subtextual meaning. For example: A secretary has a new hair style which she is very proud of and walks into her boss' office and says, "How many copies of this letter did you want?" For two years she has always made two copies. The words that are spoken are not important, but her subtext is. The secretary is actually saying, "Did you notice my new hair style?" Her physical walk, her stance, and even the way she says, "How many copies of this letter did you want?," will all be affected as she expresses the subtext (her action).

Now, of course, this is an imaginary scene from everyday life, but it could be a scene from a play. In the play the girl realizes that her boss is attractive, has a good job, a bright future and loves dogs and children. An ideal husband! Her action in the play would be to get him to propose marriage. His action may be to remain single. These actions then are the objectives of the actors. To obtain the main action or objective it is necessary for the actor to break his script down into many smaller actions similar to the secretary wanting the boss to notice her new hair style.

The action can be only physical, only thinking or a combination of both. If an actor performs his actions properly, he will avoid many of the pitfalls of the bad actor. Earlier I talked about creating emotion rather than "acting emotion" (which is impossible). We know that the "secretary" is in love with the boss. Since the play is simple, we are quite sure that the actress playing the part understands her main objective. But if she fails to prepare her smaller actions, all is lost. If she goes into the office and says her line trying to act the emotion of love the scene will become a burlesque, and even the text will become meaningless, for the boss' lines will not fit the situation. The actress indicating a love scene here would probably resort to strange posturing and weird facial expressions rather than let her own natural movements and expressions happen. Her only action for that moment must be to get him to notice her new hair style. At the same time she may be thinking—"My hair really looks good this way," or "Am I attractive now?," or "I'm prettier than the other girls working here."

Personalization

Here again we return to self, though in a slightly different way. Actors should make everything meaningful to themselves. When an actor talks about visiting a museum, they should have a specific museum they have visited in mind. If one talks about a friend or member of one's family, he or she should have a particular person in mind. If one must admire an empty canvas as if it were a great work of art, one should have a great work of art in mind. Personalizing everthing is very important to language learners. It makes them more aware of the fact that words are only the tools—the symbols and sounds—that denote ideas and objects. When we retell a story or incident our minds provide us with a movie that triggers the words. We must make sure that the movie of language learners is *not* the printed page from which they read.

Physicalization

Acting is doing. Therefore, an actor must make physical movements to help the audience understand the character's traits more completely. These physical movements will also help actors in all aspects of their acting. Imagine a situation in which an actor is portraying a rather untidy and insensitive young man waiting in a neat living room. He slouches in his chair, reaches in his pocket and opens a package of cigarettes. He drops the cellophane wrapping in the ash tray, but it falls on the table instead. He lights his cigarette and flips the match at the ash tray, but it goes over the ash tray and lands on the rug. He picks up a magazine and begins to flip through it. As he reads, the ash from his cigarette falls to the floor. Finally, the person he is waiting for arrives and he gets up tossing the magazine into the chair.

The audience knows a great deal about this character before he has said a word merely by watching his physical behavior. When working on physicalization be sure to start from self—what would I *do* in this situation?

Being very careful that your students do not tell but show which one they are doing, have them physicalize some of the following characteristics in improvisations or with "talk-and-listen" cards:

embarrassment, shyness, rudeness, nervousness,
boredom, caution, vanity, stubborness,

GEOGRAPHY AND MOVEMENTS

The director usually plans the stage movements (blocking) for the actors. Many consider this the most important job of the director. Awkward movement or no movement can be detrimental to a play, but if the actors are relaxed, communicating and fulfilling their actions, it is far more satisfying than a stage full of beautiful movements and noncommunication.

Plays generally are published in two forms, a reading version and an acting version. The acting version is the one I recommend that you use. The acting version will provide you with the basic moves that have been worked out carefully by a professional director. Also it will give a complete list of necessary properties, often a stage floor plan, and sometimes photographs and a lighting plot. Of course, if your work is only in the classroom, a lighting plot is useless, but photographs of the set, descriptions of the action, will be helpful.

If the reading edition is all that is available, or if you want to change movements from those suggested in the acting edition, there are things you should know.

The stage is divided into nine approximate areas:

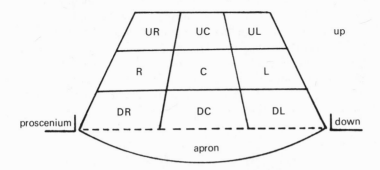

Up is away from the audience. Downstage is toward the audience. Years ago stages were raked; the upstage area was higher than down stage. Hence, up and down were used.

In the chart above, the top line would read: up right, up center, and up left. The second row would read: right, center and left. The bottom line would be: down right, down center, and down left.

You will note in acting versions that all directions are given from the actors' point of view. The reason for this is that only one person, the director, has to change left from right rather than the entire cast.

Most action of a play should be in the middle and downstage area, but, of course, the upstage section will, and should be used at times. Arrange the furniture on stage in a way that helps the actors' faces to be seen by the audience, but at the same time will look like a natural arrangement.

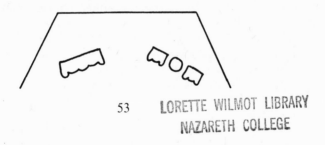

53

In the simple plan above we can see that the actors sitting in the chairs and sofa can easily talk to each other and at the same time the audience will be able to see their faces.

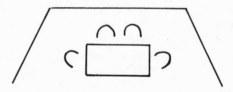

In the floor plan above with the dining table, the natural thing would be to have one chair on each side of the table, but then one of the actor's back would face the audience. If it is a long scene, this would be most distracting. The above arrangement will seem logical to the audience.

Some directors find it useful to draw miniature floor plans in the margin of their scripts with arrows indicating the moves of the actor. Generally, I only use this method when I have a large number of people on stage and want to see exact positions more clearly. Usually I mark my script with these letters and symbols.

×	cross, move, go
×DR	go down right
⊙tbl	circle the table
↓chR	sit in chair right
↑×UC	rise cross up center

If you have trouble visualizing in your mind's eye the stage movement, you might try using chessmen or other objects as actors and move them about on an enlarged floor plan of the stage area.

When you are ready for the blocking rehearsal, forget about eye contact, talk and listen, and have the actors concentrate on getting the basic moves in the scripts. Students should mark their moves on the script (*in pencil*, for there will be changes) and then execute the moves. Urge them to mark clearly to save time and confusion at later rehearsals.

Two common mistakes of the amateur actor are covering and upstaging. Both of these should be avoided by language learners, as it prevents the class or audience from seeing the faces of all the actors. The face is very expressive and helps the audience to understand the full value of the spoken word. Perhaps you have experienced the difficulty of understanding another language, or even your own, when talking over the telephone. Perfectly good speakers suddenly are very difficult to understand when you cannot see their faces.

Covering is simply a downstage actor standing in front of an upstage actor. The director can correct this easily by moving the downstage person to another position, or the upstage person can easily take a step or two left or right, so that the downstage actor is not covered.

Upstaging is when one actor is upstage of another actor, thus, forcing the downstage actor to turn his back to the audience when they are talking. In this case the director should see that actors are on an equal level.

If actor A remained in this position then both B and C would have to turn away from the audience to converse with A. If B and A move to the new position, the problem is solved. Of course there are situations when the actors should not be together, and they probably would not look at each other. In this case there would be no problem.

The main rule for blocking and movement is that it should be natural. There are, however, a number of hints the amateur actor and director can follow that will help to make a production more polished.

1. All moves must be motivated.

2. Stand facing three-quarters front (downstage) with the upstage foot slightly forward.

3. Avoid facing directly front unless you are in an upstage position.

4. Any movement on stage takes the audience's attention away from the actors who are speaking; therefore, an actor should not normally move unless he is speaking.

5. Try to time the move so the words and action coincide.

6. On entering the stage do not wait until you are in position before starting a dialogue. It should start naturally as fits the situation.

7. Most exits will be improved if the exit line is delivered on the move and finished just before exiting. A long silent move on stage delays the proceedings and weakens the exit. Again the situation may demand a long silent cross, but the actor must continue the objective.

8. Do not back into position.

9. Start your action before entering the stage; thus, you bring energy on stage. Do not start your characterization after you get on stage. The

same is true on an exit. Carry energy and hold your characterization until you are well off stage.

10. In turning on stage a turn to the audience seems less awkward than a turn away from the audience. If an actor were exiting right stage, they would exit as indicated in the diagram below.

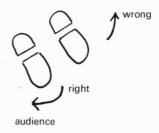

11. Kneel on downstage knee.
12. Gesture or hand props to another actor with the upstage hand.

The first one or two rehearsals after you block the play may seem terrible. This is natural. The students have lost the security of their desks or tables, and you are seeing your creation "up front" for the first time. Also, the students are trying to remember where to move, their concentration is divided. Soon all will be better than usual, for the movement will help the actors to remember their lines as well as help with their motivation and intonation. At this point you may begin to add activities, sense memory, and gesture to make the play become even more alive and natural.

Activities

There is a line attributed to a director who was having difficulty with an awkward young actor, "Don't just stand there, do something."

Often when plays are memorized by rote, especially a play in a foreign language, the actors merely stand or sit with a minimum amount of movement and recite their lines to the audience. Language learners often have a tendency to separate language and activity. In most cases the language will precede the action. As Hamlet says, "Suit the action to the word, the word to the action...." Using the "talk-and-listen" system will help the actors to communicate rather than recite; thus, making the dialogue more interesting and understandable to the audience. In real life, however, it is not too often that we just sit or stand and talk to each other. Generally, we are doing some activity. Here again concentration becomes an important part of acting. A mother preparing dinner is able to carry on a conversation with one or more persons, but her main concentration will be on preparing dinner. Her sentences will be broken in odd places, stress may come on an unusual word because of her activities, yet these do not seem strange when we see the activity that is taking place.

For the early rehearsals eye contact is stressed to aid the student to communicate. An activity will eliminate a good deal of eye contact, and the way the sentences were previously spoken, but language students can easily adapt to the new situation and become aware of their naturalness with the new language.

In the written script the playwright often gives some general activities. It is up to the actor and director to think up the many other things needed to bring the scene to life.

These are activities to try with dialogues:

Write or copy a letter, knit or sew a simple hem, solve some mathematical problems, read a newspaper (can you remember what you read?) drink a cup of tea (how annoying it is to see a drink served on stage and no one drinks it!).

Referring back to the remark, "Don't just stand there, do something." It may be wise to advise against the opposite extreme. Actors who overdo are just as unnatural when they become involved with too many activities. Such overaction can destroy a play because the audience becomes involved with the activity rather than the play.

Sense Memory

Very closely related to concentration, for it involves strong concentration on the part of the actor, is sense memory. We experience everything with our five senses. Of course, some senses are stronger than others in a given situation and, therefore, may play a more important part, but we must not overlook the others. If we bring our total sensual response to the stage, then it is much stronger and more believable than if we only indicate these responses.

If you were playing a scene that supposedly was set on the beach at sunset, what could you do to create for the audience and yourself the feeling of the beach? Remember a time when you were at the beach. First, of course, there was the sunset and water to look at; it was always changing. Was the sun very bright or could you look at it without squinting? What was the feel of the sand? Were you barefoot or were you trying to avoid sand getting into your shoes? Were you sitting with your hands in the sand letting it trickle through your fingers? What about smells—salt air, wet sand, suntan lotion, or a mixture of all three, or others? What about tastes? Had you been in the salt water or close enough to the spray to taste it? Was there the taste of suntan lotion on your lips? What were the sounds? Were the waves splashing against the beach or rocks, were people laughing and talking? Put yourself in other situations and experience all of the sensations of your five senses.

Creating the feeling of extreme heat or cold would also be helpful for sense memory. It is very easy to indicate these to the audience with the cliché actions, mopping the brow, or blowing on your hands, but the audience will not feel you are hot or cold. Remember when you were in either of these conditions and try to recall exactly how you behave and all the surrounding circumstances. Use as many of your senses to recall as you can and you will recreate that situation, so the audience will believe you.

This exercise of working without props also helps actors to be more aware of real props on stage. They help the inanimate object become alive and, therefore, receive the proper focus on stage. The careless handling of props on stage often causes actors to give wrong emphasis or importance to a prop. Actors who are afraid to touch a chair or move it so they can sit at a desk easily make the chair important because they force the body to the "will" of the chair. If an actor looks up a word in a dictionary or a number in a telephone book and opens the book with a couple of flicks of the page and locates the number or word, the audience is aware that a real dictionary or a telephone book is not being used, or that the information was memorized and did not need to be looked up. Observe what your eyes, head, fingers and possibly voice do when you look up a telephone number. These natural actions bring true life to the stage and puts the emphasis where it belongs.

Gesture

A gesture made for its own sake has no place on the stage. . . . Superfluous gestures are the same as trash, dirt, spots. . . . Let every actor above all hold his gestures in check to the extent that he controls them and not they him.

"An actor's performance which is cluttered up with a multiplicity of gestures will be like a messy sheet of paper. . . . Restraint of gesture is of particular importance in the field of characterization. . . . It often happens that an actor can find only three or four characteristic typical gestures. To be satisfied throughout a whole play with that many gestures requires utmost economy of movement. . . . Characteristic gestures cannot . . . be repeated too often or they lose their effect."

Constantin Stanislavski
An Actor's Handbook

Student actors usually are very concerned with gestures. They may practice their gestures as they memorize their lines and the result is usually an extremely mechanical performance. The foreign students are well aware that many of their gestures may be different from those of Americans and worry about performing an American play and not knowing the proper gestures.

A gesture is any movement of the body that has meaning. It is used to express an idea or to add emphasis to an expressed thought. That is more or less a dictionary explanation of gesture. Chaliapin, the great singer, gave a better explanation: "A gesture is a movement not of the body, but of the soul." Sonia Moore in writing of Stanislavski's method states, "A gesture must reflect an inner experience. It will then become a purposeful, logical, and truthful movement."

All three of these definitions point out one main idea—a gesture must have meaning. There are two types of gestures: the gesture to express a specific idea and the gesture for emphasis. The emphatic gesture is by far the most difficult to learn to control for the young actor. As a teacher/ director you are likely to discover that your biggest problem will be to get rid of the meaningless body movements that your students will have. Actually they are not completely meaningless, for what they are expressing is nervousness and insecurity. If students fulfill their duties as actors by concentrating, knowing their objectives, and their activities, these unnecessary gestures will disappear.

Probably the most common useless gesture is what has been dubbed the "high school" gesture. The elbows are held rather tightly in at the sides with either or both of the lower arms punctuating every word or two. In some cases the entire arm remains close to the side and only the hands make the frantic movements. Eliminate these gestures as soon as possible or else the body will begin to control the speech, making improvement in the flow of the language very difficult.

I do not believe in reading a line to a student for that is *my* way of saying a line. By the same token, I do not give gestures, for it would only be a copy and, therefore, not have value. The words and the gesture must come from the actor.

It is true that all people or all cultures use gestures in varying degrees. It is generally thought that Americans and Italians are very "talkative" with their hands and that the Japanese are not. However, I have had to duck from many a gesture on a Japanese subway and have seen Americans and Italians carry on long conversation without lifting a finger. It is an individual thing and if students do not ordinarily gesture then they should not gesture on stage unless they feel it.

There are those who gesture off stage well, but once on stage become awkward—the gesture is made, but they do not seem to know how to end it. The arm shoots out to accompany "Look over there," but the arm stays extended, and finally, the actor becomes aware of his arm and slowly moves it back to his side. Of course, a gesture like this is noticed and is likely to distract the audience from the play. All the actor needs to do is make the gesture and then relax the muscles and the arm will return to the side of the body as it does off stage.

Each culture has its own gestures to express various ideas or thoughts. Your students will enjoy learning these new gestures, and as part of their learning process explain feelings behind them. In time they will be able to make the gestures their own. Knowing the foreign gestures may be a great help later, and prevent embarrassment or misunderstanding, since a harmless gesture in one culture may be very rude in another.

If you are unfamiliar with foreign gestures or if there is not enough time to teach them, I feel it is permissible to allow students to use their own culture's gestures.

HISTORIES

A playwright rarely describes the past or the future of his characters, and often omits details of their present life. An actor must complete his characters biography in his mind from beginning to end, because knowing how the character grew up, what influenced his behavior, and what he expects his future to be will give more substance to the present life of the character and will give the actor a perspective and a feeling of movement in the role.

Sonia Moore
The Stanislavski System

The playwright's description of a character may be something like this: "George is a man in his forties. He dresses casually, and generally seems to be in a happy mood." Certainly there must be more to George than this or we would have a very dull character on stage. It is the job of the actor then to fill in all the details to make George a complete person, and, therefore, interesting on the stage to the audience. Go beyond the information that is available from the script and answer questions like the following:

Where did I come from?   What are my likes and dislikes?
What was my family like?   What education did I have?
What was my childhood like?   What do I think of the other
                                 characters in the play?

60

Answer questions that will help you to understand why the character behaves the way he does.

Another void in many plays is what has just happened to a character immediately before he appears on stage. Also what happens to a character when he is absent from the stage. Answer these questions:

Where did I just come from?　　Who did I see?
What was I doing?　　What did I do?

By answering these questions the actor can help make a complete performance, a circle, rather than a series of disconnected scenes.

Somewhat similar, and a very common occurrence on stage, is the telephone conversation. The actor should figure out what is being said to him and allow time for the lines to be spoken. These lines written out and actually spoken (during rehearsals) by the stage manager, or someone else, will be most helpful to the student actor. As Stanislavski said, actors should have all this information in their minds, but many actors prefer to write a "history" of the character to fill in the time that they are off stage.

For the language student I strongly recommend the written approach rather than the thought process. It gives them a chance to be creative, to express themselves in the written form, and it also gives them a stronger foundation on which to build their role. You may be amazed at the writing abilities and creativity of students when they are confronted with something that is not just another written English assignment. I have rarely made corrections of spelling, grammar, or structure on these histories. The only thing you need to check will be the logic of the background to see if it fits into the play. Of course, there are many areas of the background that will possibly have no bearing on the character's behavior in the play, such as one's favorite food, colors, hobbies, amusements, etc., but again they may.

There is no need for discussion of the various histories with other cast members as it is only meant as a foundation—the other actors must relate to what they receive on stage. Any discussion or correction should be made with the individual concerned.

For the history to have its best effect for the students, it should be written in the first person rather than the third. In this way, they identify more strongly with the character.

An unedited sample of a history written by a Japanese student who was playing a bellboy, a four-line part, in *I Remember Mama* follows:

"I was born to be the littlest boy of seven brothers and sisters. My parents were both hale and hearty and still alive. But they were so poor that I had to work. So I learned to work for a hotel of a bell boy. I, however, didn't become perverse. I had had a hope that I would be a

61

shop keeper. I wanted to have my own shop. Because my family had a little clothes shop but I wasn't be permitted to say even suggestion. At that time, I was sure that my opinion was good for them. But I didn't have a spite against them, nevertheless I learned to want to make them happy through my successes. So I am working for a hotel in good still now."

It probably took Masahiro an hour and a half to write this. Probably more is expressed in his history than his character's background. Some of his own feelings and frustrations are released. A student who becomes aware of himself will be better equipped to do anything. I am convinced that drama helps everyone to understand themselves and how they relate to others. But your concern is with language. Look at a note received from the same student seven weeks later. I asked how long it took to write and was told, "Oh, about fifteen minutes. I wrote it on the subway coming here."

"Thank you very much!!!!

"I had a very good, wonderful and impressive time at M. P. [Model Productions].

"I could become a person who likes drama a little bit. First I at least didn't like drama at all. So, this is very wonderful progress, I think. Frankly speaking, one of my purpose of my life is becoming a person who likes everything in the world. Because I want to live being surrounded by things which I love all of rather than the reverse.

"So I am sure that I could get something significant which may be able to change my life.

"Of course I could not only learn many things concerning drama that I will be able to use, but also get many wonderful friends. I want to thank you again. I never forget you. When I am asked about MP first and foremost I remember you.

Masahiro"

Is there a teacher alive who does not appreciate a paragraph like the last one? Perhaps it should be explained that the last line is a paraphrase of an important line in *I Remember Mama*, ". . . but first and foremost, I remember Mama." I, at least, am happy that he chose to remember that line.

I think you will agree that there was considerable improvement in his writing ability. Let me hasten to add that the *only* written assignment for the entire project was the history. Also there were no grammar lessons or explanations. Also I will point out that this project was being done during vacation time so no English instruction was taking place elsewhere. I do not credit Masahiro's success to me, but to drama and himself—he became involved with putting on the play, and the language learning just happened. Less than six months later he was elected president of his English-Speaking Society. And he was not the only one to improve; they all made remarkable improvement.

The following two histories were written by American T.E.S.O.L. students at the University of Hawaii for plays they were performing. The bus driver is a character in the short play, *People in the Wind* by William Inge. The other is Sam from Thornton Wilder's *The Long Christmas Dinner*—it too is a very short role, three lines, but the actor developed him into a complete person.

THE BUS DRIVER

Al Hoel

I was born outside of Kansas City on a small farm in 1925. I was the oldest of six children. We were a poor but happy family. We dutifully attended the local Methodist church every Sunday, even in the worst of weather. My parents, poor and tired though they were, raised us in an upright and moral way. I guess I've not been the best of sons, but I still respect my parents and what they tried to teach me.

I never liked school, and so in the seventh grade I called it quits and helped my father on the farm full time. When I was about sixteen I grew tired of the hard work on the farm. I didn't want to grow up looking old and wrinkled before my time, so I headed for Kansas City to make my fortune.

I soon realized that fortunes were hard to come by, and took a job washing dishes in a grubby cafe. A year or so later I graduated to driving buses. I had to lie about my age in order to get the job, but since I looked older than I really was, I got it without any trouble.

I've quite the job a couple of times since then and have gone into other lines of work, like selling washing machines and loading freight cars. But, I always came back sooner or later. I guess bus driving is in my blood. I liked the freedom of the road. When you're driving the bus, you're the captain. Nobody's going to tell you what to do.

I've been working pretty steadily now for the last ten years, driving the Greyhound between Kansas City and Wichita. Having a wife and two kids forces a guy to settle down and think more about security. I'll probably keep driving this route until I drop dead behind the wheel some lonely, windy night.

ACT II

SOME NOTES ON MY LIFE

Randal Hongo

I was born Samuel Morrison Bayard on December 29, 1900, the son—I had a twin sister—of Charles and Leonora Bayard. Mother and father named me Samuel after a king in the Old Testament. They told me that their parents had regretted not giving them Christian names, so they hoped to compensate for this shortcoming by naming me Samuel. It was not an act of deep religious conviction, I'm sure. My twin sister was named Lucia, and my younger brother was named Roderick. I may not be a Bible expert, but I don't recall ever seeing either of those names in either the Old or New Testaments.

Staunton, Virginia had always been my home. It's a fair-sized town set in the greenest part of the Shenandoah Valley. The population when I left was about 25,000 and father's lumber company was one of the biggest in Staunton.

Father always reminded us that we were of "the first family of this city!" I can still hear his voice booming across the dinner table, reminding us to behave in public and to remember our position in the town's society. I never agreed much with father's philosophies. His business made him almost inhuman at times; all he thought about was the firm, the factory and our status in the community. Mother was of gentler, more human stock—as mothers should be. She rounded off father's rough corners. In her unassuming way, she was both father's adviser and his faithful subordinate. She was a loving person and made life at home wonderful for everyone. I was closer to Lucia although we did have our moments of hassling. She especially got annoyed when I teased her about the boys she met at the country club dances father made us attend. Rod was the typical brother—all questions, all eyes and ears, all pestering hands.

I remember our house as clearly as when I used to stand in front of it on summer afternoons, staring at the huge, overbearing edifice with its rusty ironwork filigree, off-white bordered windows and fading green skin. It looked like a cumbersome, lazy animal sitting there in the heat of summer. Mother and father loved that house, and told us many times that it represented—though I never asked how—the many generations of the Bayard family.

Some of my best memories of life at home were from that last summer I spent there before going off to Europe. Meeting Beth Anderson at the country club dance was the highlight of my whole life. For once, I had met a girl who wasn't a class-conscious snob—who didn't care what my father did for a living or whether I had been out to California or not. I really liked her a lot. We saw each other quite regularly after that, hiking up to Manassah Falls and to the Blue Ridge Lookout Point. She came to dinner at our house twice, and I knew that mother and father took a liking to her, too.

It was Beth who introduced me to stamp-collecting. At first, I thought it boring to hunt around for out-of-date faded blue 4¢ stamps. But Beth had an enthusiasm about her that made everything she did seem exciting. In a matter of days, I had become converted.

I found some really interesting stamps that I pasted in an album that I was planning to give Beth. But by late August, for a number of reasons that are still hazy, we stopped seeing each other. She told me she planned to go off to college in Maine in October and would be "busy" the rest of the time planning for her big move. I tried to understand. I never did get to give Beth those stamps. But I kept the album tucked inconspicuously among other books on my desk, and it always had some special meaning for me.

I don't know what made me sign up that November. The newspapers were hinting that there might be big trouble in Europe; some government people boldly predicted that war would eventually break out. I had no immediate plans for my life. I graduated from Lee High School that past June and didn't want to enter college right away. Serving my country would be a good diversion for awhile, I thought. Besides, it would be a way of forgetting Beth.

As expected, father was proud. It was a good thing to do, he said. I'm confident it was paternal pride that made him beam—as well as the joy that I was upholding the Bayard name in Staunton, of course.

They took me in a matter of weeks and I was to report for basic training on the twentieth of December, just a few days before my 19th birthday. Mother threw a party for me—a combination birthday-bon-voyage-Christmas celebration. I remember that I wished Beth had been there. But it was a foolish thought and one that I soon forgot amidst the laughter and merriment.

The Bayards never went in for long goodbyes. But if I had known I was never to see them again, I might have said more to my family. And maybe even hugged father. But young men should be brave little stoics and without emotion. So I was. For an instant, perhaps, I may have betrayed the heaviness I felt deep inside at leaving my family and home—forever, as it turned out to be.

Special Problems

Stage Embrace

Kissing on stage is very common and can be a problem with amateur actors. First, it is important to remember that it is acting, that it is not real, but must look real. Many young people are embarrassed to kiss in front of others and want to delay rehearsing the kiss as long as possible (some say "Oh, we'll do it the night of the performance"). Just as with a difficult scene, the sooner you start work on it the better. Start rehearsing embraces as soon as the students stop using their scripts. If the actors rehearse it, they will not be embarrassed when they perform, and the audience will be relaxed and accept it, rather than laugh and giggle.

Actors must be relaxed and well balanced when they embrace on stage. The feet should be placed as illustrated below. The bodies should be close together, not just the heads. The man's downstage arm should be about the woman's waist, and his upstage arm around her shoulders. The woman's downstage arm should rest on his arm and her upstage arm just under his. As they kiss their bodies may take a slight twist up stage.

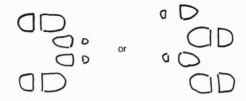

If an actor is "stealing" a kiss or giving his partner a surprise kiss, then, of course, he would do just that, but it too should be rehearsed. Other kisses such as those among family or friends can be on the cheek. Among two women, two cheeks touching is an affectionate greeting and may be used instead of a kiss. Parents, husbands, wives, and children often kiss on top of the head if the other party is seated and they are standing. This would be especially fitting before saying good night or on returning home.

Slaps and Fights

Like the kiss, the slap must be rehearsed as soon as possible in order that no damage is done. A stage slap is a real slap; it is not faked. Done properly no damage will be done, but it will sting. There are a number of things that can be done to make it safe and perhaps less painful.

Actors being slapped should remain relaxed, their mouths closed, but teeth separated. Be sure not to clench the teeth or tighten the jaw. As the hand touches the face the head turns slightly moving with the hand. Be careful not to anticipate and turn too soon or the slap may land on the ear, which may be dangerous, and the ringing sensation will be annoying and uncomfortable.

The person doing the slapping must look where they are going to slap. Do not wear rings. The slap should be made with the hand open and relaxed, the fingers, not the palm, hitting the fleshy part of the cheek. Follow through with the slap. Do not hit and stop. Caution: look where you are hitting to avoid eyes, ears, and nose. The slap should be rehearsed carefully and slowly apart from the regular rehearsal as well as in the rehearsal itself, until the actors become well coordinated. The slap should make a good sound which will have the proper effect on the audience. The sting of the slap will help both actors in creating the proper emotion.

Fights are not as common on stage as they are in movies. In movies they are usually performed by stunt men. A stage fight might consist of a couple of hits and then a struggle. These scenes should be rehearsed apart from the regular rehearsal and each move planned very carefully. A very definite plan needs to be worked out and repeated the same way at each rehearsal and performance. Naturally a punch must be pulled just before landing on the jaw or chin of an actor to avoid injury. Grunts and groans from the struggling actors will aid the effect, and if other actors are on stage perhaps one can slap his hands together or the side of his leg just as a punch 'connects." Of course, this must be unnoticed by the audience. Usually I gave these simple instructions to the students involved and told them to work it out. I was never disappointed.

Drunkenness

Most of us have a stereotype idea of a drunk which we use in telling jokes or when we are kidding around with our friends. This stereotype is very likely to be used on stage for it indicates drunkenness immediately to the audience. Avoid this trap. Performing in this cliche manner destroys the reality of the performance. Alcohol affects everyone differently, and people get drunk for different reasons. Students should study the situation, the character, and themselves to develop a truthful interpretation.

Crying and Laughing

Crying and laughing are likely to sound artificial on stage. Students should not rely on the printed "ha-ha-ha" or "boo-hoo" for the correct sound. These are usually used only to indicate laughing or crying. Again, students should study the situation to discover the motivation for the behavior. If the student is involved in the situation the resulting laugh or cry will be correct.

Accents

It is not necessary to add an accent to denote a person from a particular locality or country. The purpose of the play is to teach English, therefore the students should speak the best English they can. Students will naturally have their own accents, they should not complicate matters by trying to add another.

Facial Expressions

Students should not learn facial expressions. The proper facial expression will occur when the students are involved in the situation.

Jerry D. Boucher of the Culture Learning Institute of the East-West Center has recently completed a study of facial expressions of various cultures. In his paper he says, "... there is definitely a relationship between what a person is feeling, what he can show on his face, and what people think he is feeling .... facial expressions of emotion are the same in at least the more than 20 different cultures studied: when a person is feeling sad and is making no attempt to camouflage his feelings, he has the same facial expression whether he lives in North America, Japan, New Guinea, or Malaysia."

The six plays that follow are simple to do and to understand. They can be easily performed in the classroom and take about fifteen minutes each to perform. They are intended for you and your students to use as starters before attempting plays from the suggested list.

Plays for the Classroom

NEVER ON WEDNESDAY is a look at an average family in the United States. The conversation is very informal and includes a lot of teasing among the young people. Tom, in fact, even mimics his father. Most of the conversation is the type that might be repeated daily. The humor comes from seeing ourselves in a natural situation. With rewriting the roles of Fred and Tom may be played by girls.

NEVER ON WEDNESDAY

Richard Via

CAST

Fred	about 17 years old
Dorothy (Dot)	about 16 years old
Tom	about 14 years old
Dad	40–45 years old
Mother	38–43 years old

SETTING: The action takes place in the living room of a "typical" American family. Dad is reading the evening newspaper and is sitting in a chair to the right of a lamp table on stage right. Dorothy is in the chair to the left of this table and is busily manicuring her fingernails. The sound of the nail file as it scratches back and forth bothers Tom, who is trying to do his homework. Tom is seated at a table behind the sofa on stage left. Fred is stretched out on the sofa reading a comic book. Mother is off stage right, in the kitchen.

TIME: Just after dinner (supper)—7:30 P.M.

AT RISE: We watch the quiet scene for a few moments. Then the phone rings in the hall off stage left. Both Dot and Fred react quickly. Both jump to answer it, but Fred is nearer and quicker. They speak as they get up, and at the same time. Fred thinks it's his girl friend and Dot thinks it's her boy friend calling.

Fred: I'll get it. (*Goes to door and exits to the hall*)
Dot: Ooooh! I think it's for me.
   (*She returns to the table to put the nail file down*)
Dot: Tell him I'll be there in a sec.
   (*She looks at the hall door, expecting to be called to the phone. When she isn't, she sits and starts working on her nails again. Dad and Tom pay no attention to any of this activity*)

Tom: (*without looking up*) Tell her I'm busy. Ask her to leave her number.

(*We hear Fred talking in the hall on the phone, but we cannot understand what he is saying*)

Fred: (*standing in the doorway*) Dad, can I use the car tonight?

Tom: (*imitating Dad*) No.

Fred: (*goes to the left end of the sofa*) Would you be quiet?

Tom: You'll see..."No."

Fred: (*to Tom—annoyed*) Don't put ideas in his head.

(*Goes to Dad's right. Starts talking at first step*)—

Dad, can I have the car tonight?

Dad: Uhmmm?

Fred: (*slightly upset that Dad didn't listen*) I said, "Can I use the car tonight?"

Dad: (*correcting Fred's English*) May I....

Fred: Okay. *May* I?

Dad: May you what?

Fred: (*really annoyed with the older generation—perhaps throws his arms up in disgust*) You mean you really didn't hear anything I said except "can I"?

(*Goes behind Dad to center stage*)

Dot: (*actually teasing Dad rather than Fred*) Haven't you heard of the generation gap? They turn us *off*.

Dad: Not as often as you turn *us* off.

Fred: You *heard that*—and she wasn't even *talking* to you.

(*Goes back to Dad's left*)

Why don't you hear *me*?

Dot: (*teasing Fred*) It's your deep voice. It doesn't carry.

Tom: It won't carry through that scratching you're making with that nail file.

Dot: (*teasing Tom because he bites his fingernails*) At least I don't bite my nails—like some people do.

Tom: (*imitating nail-file noise—this sound should be loud and exaggerated*) Grrgh-grrgh. I can't even do my homework.

Fred: (*goes to center again*) Would you two cut it out? I'm trying to reach Dad.

(*Goes to Dad's left, behind the lamp table*)

Dad?

Dad: (*without looking up*) Uhmmm?

Fred: Dad?

(*Trying to make him listen, he stretches the word, Da-a-a-d—perhaps almost sings it. Then, as if trying to contact a spirit:*)

Dad, give us a sign you're listening: one rap for Yes,
(raps on table once)
two for No.
(raps twice)

Dad: *(putting the paper down)* Okay, you got through. What is it?

Fred: Whew! *(a sound like letting off steam, indicating relief)*
(Goes to Dad's right)
Dad, may I use the car tonight?

Dad: No. *(Goes back to paper)*

Fred: Wait!! Don't hang up! *(as if Dad were on the phone)*. I'm not finished.

Tom: *(smiles as he goes to the bookcase up center for a book)* I told you so.
(Mother enters and listens to this bit of dialogue, Tom returns to the table)

Fred: Back to your books, Einstein. *(Goes to right center)*

Mother: Fred, I've told you about that.
(Goes to the sofa, sits at the right end, and picks up knitting or sewing from the coffee table)
Rather than tease Tom, you'd better do a little studying yourself.

Dot: Do you like this color, Mother? *(Shows her fingernails)*

Mother: You shouldn't do your nails in the living room, dear. They should only be done in the privacy of one's boudoir.

Dot: *(simultaneously)*....in the privacy of one's boudoir. *(Said with a bored sound, because she's heard this so many times)*

Mother: Yes. And Tom, why don't you study in your room?

Tom: This is where the action is—it's too quiet up there.

Dot: Mother. *(Goes to Mother)*
You didn't answer me. Do you like this color?

Mother: Very pretty.

Dot: *(going back to chair)* It's new...a special color for this month: Passion Pink.

Tom: *(teasing Dot, imitates the girls in TV commercials)* "And my hair color is special this month: Blatant Black."

Dot: *(not thinking he's funny)* Oh, you're so funny.
(Not laughing, but flat:)
Ha, ha, ha....

Mother: By the way, where was all that help I was going to have in the kitchen with the dishes?

Tom: I had to do homework.

Dot: And my nails.

Fred: I've been trying to talk to Dad.

73

Mother: You kids are really great at finding excuses. Homework isn't so urgent when the Rolling Stones are on TV, and nails can stop when there's someone to gossip with on the phone.
(*Slight pause—then*:)

Tom: (*pokes his mother's back*) What about Fred? Why don't you attack him?

Mother: Well...when a son wants to talk to his father, that's important.

Fred: I thought so, too. (*Goes to the sofa and sits down*)

Mother: What did you two talk about?

Fred: Nothing.

Mother: Nothing?

Fred: He said about ten words. (*Indicates newspaper*) I can't crash the newspaper barrier.

Mother: Paul?

(*Dad puts the paper down immediately. He has been well trained by Mother to listen to her when she speaks*)

Dad: Yes, dear?

Tom: That's training!

Mother: (*to Tom*) Do you want to leave the room?

(*Tom shakes his head No*)

Mother: Then behave youself.

Dad: Yes, dear? You wanted me?

Mother: No, Paul. Fred wanted to talk to you.

(*Fred starts to go to Dad, gets to center*)

Dad: Oh, that. (*He starts reading again—paper up*)

Fred: (*turns back to Mother*) You see! *That!* He refers to me as "that"!

Mother: Don't get so upset....He's tired. Paul?

Dad: (*paper down*) Yes, dear?

Mother: (*signaling Fred to go to Dad*) Now, go ahead.

Fred: (*quickly*) Dad, may I....(*Goes quickly to Dad's right*)

Dad: No. (*Paper up*)

Fred: (*to Dad*) Wait. (*Goes back to center. To Mother*:) You see?

Mother: (*rises, goes to Fred*) What was it you wanted to talk to him about?

Dad: (*paper down*) He wants to use the car. (*Paper up*)

Mother: (*goes to Dad's right*) Well, why can't he?

Dad: (*paper down*) It's Wednesday. (*Paper up*)

Mother: Yes, it's Wednesday.

Dot: You don't need a calendar in this house. You just ask Dad for the car and he tells you what day it is.

Mother: (*goes behind table near Dot*) Dorothy, that's not nice.

Dot: Well, it's true. Yesterday *I* asked and he said, "No, it's Tuesday."

74

Dad: (*paper down*) You know the rules.

(*Speaking together*:)

{ Fred: Yes, we know the rules. Weekends only.
  Tom: Yes, you may only use the car on weekends.
  Dot: Do we ever! Friday, Saturday, and Sunday afternoon.

Dad: (*paper up*) Right.

Mother: (*to Fred*) What did you want the car for?

Dad: (*paper down*) I said No. (*Paper up*)

Mother: Now, don't be so harsh. Maybe there's a special reason for him needing the car.

Dad: (*paper down*) A rule's a rule. (*Paper up*)

(*Tom mouths the above line as Dad says it, but makes no sound*)

Mother: (*goes to Fred*) Where were you going?

Tom: (*guessing why he wants the car and teasing*)
To a drive-in movie with that new girl.

Dot: (*referring to the new girl*) She bleaches her hair, you know.

Fred: She does not.

Mother: (*disappointed in Fred, goes to the sofa and sits down*) You want the car to date on a week night?

Fred: No!

(*Very annoyed with Tom, he goes to him and musses his hair*)
See what you started. Why don't you grow up?

Mother: Now, boys (*meaning, Don't start a fight*). What *did* you want the car for, Fred?

Fred: Well, it's a secret.

Dot: (*comes back to center*) It *was* her, though, wasn't it? As soon as you hung up you came in and asked Dad for the car.

Tom: I don't go with girls who call me.

(*Rises, stretches. His back is tired from doing homework*)
I call them. I'm going to be the boss and make the decisions. No girl's going to run my life.

(*Sits down*)

Fred: Some boss! Every time you call a girl, she hangs up on you.

Tom: (*very strong, defending his manhood*) That's not so! (*Meaning: That's not true*)

Mother: Let's not start again. Now both of you, be quiet.

Fred: Look, Mom. (*Goes back to the sofa, sits down*)
I really need the car. Honest.

Mother: Don't you think you ought to tell us where you're going?

Fred: Can't you trust me? It's a surprise.

Tom: (*almost laughing—teasing Fred*) Yeah, I bet. (*Meaning: I'm sure it will be a surprise!*)

75

We were surprised that time you smashed the left fender, too.
(*Takes book back to shelf*)

Fred: (*disgusted*) Oh, forget it. (*Starts for door left*) I'll go by taxi.
(*The word "taxi" makes Dad listen*)

Dad: (*paper down*) To a drive-in movie?

Fred: I told you I'm not going to a movie. (*Comes back a step*)

Dad: Well, a taxi anywhere will be expensive.

Fred: I have to go, and you won't let me use the car.

Dad: All right. Then let's talk it over. What's so urgent?
(*Puts paper on table*)

Mother: He said it was a secret.

Fred: A surprise.

Dad: And you can't tell us what it is?

Dot: I'm going to use that technique the next time I want something.

Dad: I haven't said Yes yet.

Mother: Don't you think you could let him this time, Paul?

Dad: How long will you want it?

Fred: If I don't hurry, I won't need it at all. Grandma's at the station....

Mother: (*rises*) Grandma?!

Fred: Yes! She said she'd take a taxi, but I said I'd be right down....
Oh my gosh, she's still on the phone!
(*He rushes into the hall*)

Dad: (*gets up*) Why didn't she let us know?

Mother: Fred said she wanted to surprise us.
(*Fred returns*)

Dad: You'd better get moving.

Dot: Can I ride down with you? (*Goes to door left*)

Tom: Me, too. (*Closes books and goes to the door*)

Mother: What about your homework and your nails?

Dot: They're okay. (*Exits*)

Tom: I'll do it later. (*Exits*)

Mother: Hurry, dear. What are you waiting for?

Fred: The keys.

Dad: Oh...oh, sorry. (*Goes to Fred, hands him the keys*) Now drive careful.

Mother: (*correcting Dad's English*) Careful*ly* (*with strong stress on the last syllable*).

Dad: Yes, dear. (*He watches them leave*)

Mother: Now why didn't she let me know she was coming? She knows I like to have things ready.
(*Mother picks up a comic book and the sewing from the sofa and coffee table. She goes to the chair right and picks up the newspaper, then to the lamp table and picks up all the manicure stuff*)

Dad: (*as he crosses to his chair to resume reading*) If she let you know, you'd get all worked up about everything....
(*He can't find his paper*)
    ...cooking...cleaning...Tom's hair....
(*He suddenly sees that Mother has the paper and goes to her for it*)
Mother: (*who now is picking up all of Tom's books and papers and putting everything in the bookcase*) But she should have called. Suppose we'd been away?
Dad: (*gets his paper*) In the middle of the week? With the kids in school and me at work? Not likely!
(*Meaning that, since he must be at work and the children are in school, it is not likely that the family would be out of town*)
Mother: Just the same (*meaning even if that is true*), I wish I'd known.
Dad: (*sits down*) No communication....
(*hunts for what he was reading*)
    ...generation gap....
(*he finds it*)
    ...only at the other end of the line.
(*Meaning that there is a generation gap not only between parents and children but also between parents and grandparents*)
(*Paper up—Dad reads. Mother continues to straighten things up as the curtain falls*)

CURTAIN

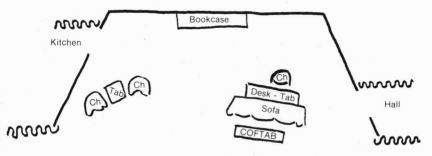

Never on Wednesday

THE NOW depicts another typical family in the United States. This time, however, the younger generation uses the language of today. This language and the very informal behavior shows the generation gap that exists.

Usually the use of a slang expression by a nonnative speaker sounds inappropriate unless he is very fluent. However, students need to understand slang when they hear or read it. Also I have found that most students enjoy learning these new expressions for it helps them to identify with their counterparts in the U.S.

The roles of the three boys may be rewritten to be played by three girls.

THE NOW

Richard Via

CAST

Matt	A friend	Age 15–18
Paul		15–18
Joe		13–16
Mom }	The Family	35–40
Dad		40–45

SCENE: The living room of the Finley home. It is about 6 P.M. The room is neat and clean except for several empty coke bottles, plastic wrappers, cookie boxes, comic books, loose records, and record jackets scattered about.

AT RISE: Matt is slouching in the chair on stage right with his legs extended far into the room. His eyes are closed and one arm is moving in tempo with the loud rock music coming from the phonograph. Paul is stretched out on the sofa as if asleep. Joe is lying on the floor reading a comic book. The music continues for about two minutes.

Matt: Play that part again.
Paul: What?
Matt: I said play that section again.
Paul: Man, you got to speak up. I can't hear you.
  (*Matt gets up and steps over Joe and stops the record. When the music stops, both Joe and Paul react by sitting up suddenly*)
Paul: Hey, what are you doing?
Matt: Nothing. I just want to hear that section again. They're groovy.
Paul: Yeah. They're out-a-sight.
Matt: Listen.
  (*The record starts again. Matt starts to move or dance with the music with his eyes closed. Paul and Joe go back to their original positions. Mom enters from the kitchen*)

Mom: Paul?....Paul, would you turn that thing down?

(She gets no response so steps over Joe and turns the phonograph off. Matt stops dancing and opens his eyes. Paul sits up suddenly)

Paul: Hey, man, what's coming off?....Oh, Mom....you....

Mom: Yes, it's me.

Matt: Hello, Mrs. Finley.

Mom: Hello, Matt. How are your folks?

Matt: Okay, I guess.

Mom: That's nice. *(in center stage)* Paul, would you and Joe straighten up this room a bit? Your father will be home soon....

Joe: *(as he looks about the room)* What's the matter with the room?

Paul: Yeah, the pad's straight.

Mom: It looks better than *your* pig pen, but it's hardly straight. I'll bet your living room never looks like this, does it, Matt?

Matt: Yeah. Maybe. I don't know....Mom's so fussy. Not like you.

Mom: Thanks for the compliment, but Mr. Finley *is* fussy, so you'd better get busy, boys. *(She starts for the kitchen)*

Joe: What....what's to do? *(What is there to do?)*

Mom: *(pointing out things)* Put the records back in their jackets and take them to your room. Take these coke bottles and empty cookie boxes to the kitchen....*(She is now by the coffee tables and sees a cigarette butt in the ashtray)*....Who's been smoking?

(There is a moment's fear)

Joe: Must be Dad's.

Mom: It is not your father's. I emptied all the ashtrays this morning. Paul, have you been smoking?

Matt: It was me, Mrs. Finley....

Mom: Does your mother know you smoke?

Matt: *(avoiding the issue)* Well....I think so....I'm not sure.

Mom: Do you smoke at home?

Matt: No, ma'm. I guess I'd better be going.

Paul: Oh, stick around a while. I want to tell you something.

Mom: Well, your father will be home soon. I'm just warning you. *(She exits into the kitchen)*

Joe: What a drag!

Paul: *(when he's sure Mom cannot hear)* Put it here. *(shakes hands)* Matt, thanks for taking the rap for me. Anybody got a stick of gum? *(Joe gives him two pieces which he hurriedly puts in his mouth to cover the tobacco breath. He says the next line as he unwraps the gum)* They're hung up on my smoking.

Matt: Mine too....gosh, both my parents smoke like chimneys! But they'd kill me if I smoked. I hope your mom doesn't telephone my mom.

Joe: Mom's neat. She won't call, but Dad. . . . that's another scene.

Paul: I really don't see what's so great about smoking anyway.

Joe: It must taste good or something, or else why would so many people smoke?

Paul: Well, I didn't taste *anything*. (*pause*) Maybe I'll *stop* smoking.

Joe: Cop out! You've only had one!

Paul: I know, but. . . . well, Dad. . . . and it's expensive, fifty cents a pack. . . . You want this pack, Matt? (*offers him the pack*)

Matt: No, thanks, if my parents found them in my room. . . . it'd be the third degree.

Joe: Give 'em to me. I want to try 'em.

Paul: (*tossing him the pack*) Okay, but don't blame me if you get caught. I'll deny everything.

Joe: Gee, thanks!

Matt: I'd better split.

(*He starts for the door and gets there just as Dad enters. Joe quickly puts the cigarettes in his pocket. Dad puts his briefcase on the phonograph*)

Dad: Hello, Matt. How are you?

Matt: Okay, I guess, Mr. Finley.

Dad: You don't know? (*Don't you know?*)

Matt: Don't know what?

Dad: How you are.

Joe: (*to Dad*) Come off it.

Matt: (*to Dad*) What do you mean?

Dad: Well, I asked you how you were and you said, "Okay, I guess."

Matt: Oh. . . . yeah. . . . Well, I'd better go. So-long.

Joe and Paul: So-long.

Dad: So-long, Matt.

Paul: Dad, why do you do that?

Dad: What?

Paul: Talk that way. Why don't you get with it? You always try to confuse my friends.

Joe: Yeah. Mine too.

Dad: I'm not trying to confuse them. I just want you to learn to speak up and give a proper answer.

Paul: But, Dad, that's the old way. It's old fashioned. We talk different-ly now. This is the *now* generation.

Dad: Well, *now* is the time to learn how to behave, and *now* is the time to clean up this room. NOW. (*He sits in the chair right*)

Paul: (*disgusted*) Oh, you can't win.

Joe: Old people!

Dad: What's that?

Joe: Nothing.

(*The boys start to pick up everything. Dad starts to read the paper. Mother comes in*)

Mom: Oh, I thought I heard you come in. Have a good day?

Dad: Yes, until *now*.

(*The boys exit into kitchen. Both give Dad a dirty look*)

Mom: What's the matter? Headache?

Dad: No, the boys. They seem to resent it when I come home. I feel like I'm not wanted.

Mom: (*trying to soothe him*) Oh, that's not so, and you know it. We *all* love you.

Dad: Well, I *wish* they'd show it.

Mom: They're at that age. Don't you remember when you were their age?

Dad: I never acted like that.

Mom: No, I'm sure you didn't, but I'm sure you felt your father didn't understand you.

Dad: Well, I don't remember it.

Mom: Now, Bill, think....didn't you ever sneak out behind the barn and smoke corn silk?

Dad: (*relaxing and chuckling*) Well, now that you mention it....I did. I got the beating of my life when my father caught me. I'll never forget that.

Mom: There, you see.

Dad: It's a wonder I ever took up smoking after that. (*He stops and gets serious*) Say, those boys haven't been smoking, have they? If they have, I'll....

Mom: Bill, calm down. No, they haven't. I found one cigarette butt in the ash tray, and Matt said he had been smoking.

Dad: Well, I don't want him smoking in my house.

Mom: All right, Bill, I'll speak to the boys about it.

(*Joe and Paul enter from kitchen*)

Joe: About what?

Paul: Speak to us about what?

Mom: Nothing important. We'll talk later.

Dad: No, we might as well talk now.

Mom: (*firmly*) *Bill*, I said *I'd* do it. Now, let's not get into this before dinner. It's almost ready.

Joe: Gee, Dad, you're up tight. Keep your cool.

THE NOW

Dad: (*annoyed*) What's that? What are you talking about?

Paul: Up tight. You know, nervous, tense, inhibited....tight.

Dad: It's no wonder we can't communicate. You can't even speak English.

Joe: It's English! The *now* English. You're just not with it.

Dad: "With it"?

Paul: "In." You don't keep up with the times. You don't understand, see?

Dad: Is that the kind of English you're learning at school?

Joe: Naw, (*no*) most of the teachers are like you, kind of freaky.

Mom: (*interrupting to save the day*) Well, I'm going to lose my cool if all of you don't get with it and get ready for dinner.

Joe: Gee. Mom, you're one of the beautiful people. You're with it.

Paul: I'm ready to eat.

Mom: Did you wash your hands?

Paul: (*annoyed*) What do you think we are....kids?

Mom: Yes, I do. Look at Joe's hands. They're filthy.

Joe: That's not dirt! It's just grease from my bicycle.

Mom: (*ending the discussion*) WASH!

Joe: Okay, okay....Keep your cool.

(*Joe and Paul exit up to hallway*)

Mom: Bill, you can go on in and start serving the plates.

Dad: I may be too nervous to digest my food.

Mom: Oh, Bill, you take it all too seriously.

Dad: It is serious.

Mom: I know, but they'll turn out all right. They're testing their independence....finding a little privacy with their "now" language as they call it. We did the same thing.

Dad: We talked in English and our songs made sense, not all that loud rock stuff.

Mom: Did they, Bill? Do you remember "Mairzy doats and dozy doats and little lamzy divy"?

Dad: (*warming up*) My, gosh, you're right. I guess I shouldn't blow my stack or I won't sleep when I hit the sack.

(*Paul and Joe enter up left and stay in the doorway listening to Mom and Dad*)

Mom: Oh, my yes, and jive.

(*Mom dances a bit. Mom and Dad laugh*)

Dad: Hey, bob-a-ree-bop!

(*Again, they laugh*)

Paul: Hey, I dig it. What is it?

Dad: Oh, just a little of the "then" generation talk.

THE NOW

Mom: Does it grab you? Come on, let's put on the feed bag.
   (*They all start for the kitchen*)
Joe: Gee. Mom, did you really use to talk that way?

CURTAIN

"Now" vocabulary
   Man—vocative
   groovy—good
   out-a-sight—good
   what's coming off?—What's happening?
   pad—room, apartment, living quarters
   What a drag—boring
   put it here—a slapping of palms, hand shake
   hung up—too involved, too concerned
   neat—good
   scene—place, situation
   cop out—quitter
   third degree—dirty looks, the brush off, stern talk
   split—leave, go
   come off it—stop teasing, quit kidding
   get with it—understand
   up tight—tense
   in—something or someone who is up to date
   freaky—strange, out of date
   one of the beautiful people—someone who understands
   to dig—to understand, to like
   to grab—to interest
   keep your cool—remain calm

"Then" vocabulary
   "Mairzy doats and dozy doats and little lamzy divy"—a song which meant
      "Mares eat oats, and does eat oats, and little lambs eat ivy."
   blow my stack—get angry
   hit the sack—go to bed
   jive—jazz or swing music
   hey, bob-a-ree-bop—jive talk that was used in many songs
   put on the feed bag—to eat

THE NOW

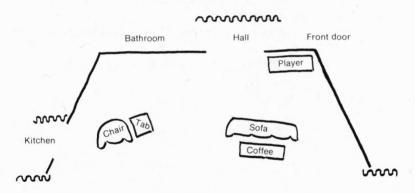

The Now

CRASH. In the beginning the dialogue is most informal as the students are not being too serious about the museum. After the accident when the young people must deal with the guard and Mr. Smithers the conversation becomes more formal.

Crash may be easily played by an all-male or all-female cast.

CRASH

Richard Via

CAST

Joan
Peter
Matt
Guard (George)
Mr. Smithers

SETTING: A room in a museum. There are doorways on stage right and left leading to other galleries. An archway or another door up center goes to a main hallway. The walls have paintings or other art objects on them. Left center is a pedestal with a vase or bowl on it. Right center is a bench or chairs for resting and viewing.

TIME: Saturday morning.

AT RISE: The stage is empty. Almost immediately we hear someone laughing off stage right, and Joan, Peter, and Matt enter. Peter is still laughing and Joan is trying to quiet him.

Joan: Sh, sh, they'll throw us out.
Peter: I can't help it.
Matt: I still don't see what's so funny.
Peter: That piece of junk in there. (*Indicating the room they just left*) They think that's art?
Joan: Did it ever occur to you that perhaps you just don't understand it.
Peter: And you wanna know something. I don't want to understand it.
Matt: Well I don't like it either, but I don't see any point of making a....
Peter: (*interrupting*) Because you're afraid to express your true feelings.
Matt: I don't think that kooky laughter expressed your true feeling— it was just an act....
(*Peter is ready to answer when a guard comes in the archway*)

CRASH

Guard: Would you keep your voices down.

Peter: Okay Mac.

(*The guard is a little annoyed with the curt reply, but decides to ignore it and exits*)

Joan: See—I told you.

(*They move about in different directions looking at the paintings*)

Matt: Hey Joan.

Joan: Yeah.

Peter: (*making fun*) Sh, sh, I'm observing the art.

Matt: (*gives him a look then to Joan*) Art test. (*He covers the name of the artist with his hand*) who did this?

Joan: (*goes over to him—Peter goes to the pedestal, left center*) You! (*She laughs*)

Matt: How'd you guess? No, seriously.

Joan: Monet or Renoir I think—Monet?

Matt: Very good!! (*He removes his hand*)

Joan: You freak—(*Jokingly annoyed since the artist was neither of those named*)

Peter: (*rather excited*) Hey you guys—take a look at this.

Matt: (*turning toward Peter*) What?

Peter: This vase—now this is art!

Joan: (*as they cross to him*) You're putting us on again.

Peter: No, I'm not—I really think it's great.

Matt: Yeah, it's nice, but what's it for?

Peter: It doesn't have to be *for* anything.

Joan: Maybe it was a funeral urn, or an incense burner, or....

Peter: Look at the shape—and the color. (*He touches the vase—tests its thickness*) And the thickness—really amazing they could do that kind of work that long ago.

Joan: (*being corny*) If only this vase could talk, what tales it could tell.

Matt: Rub the side and see if a genie appears.

Peter: Oh, cut it out—you've got no sensitivity.

Matt: You weren't so sensitive in the other room.

Peter: Okay you made your point. (*He really is so attracted to the vase that he picks it up to feel the weight and texture*)

Joan: Are you crazy—put that down.

Matt: Yeah—can't you read—(*he reads sign*) "Do not touch."

Peter: I'll be careful—but pottery should be felt to really appreciate it. (*Joan and Matt are concerned about him holding it. Matt turns quickly to see if the guard is near. As he turns, he accidentally bumps Pete's arm and the vase crashes to the floor. There is a moment of stunned silence as they all three look at the vase*)

Peter: Damn, what did you do that for?

CRASH

Matt: Do what?

Peter: Hit my arm like that.

Joan: It was an accident Pete.

Matt: Yeah, I was just checking to see if that guard was around.

Peter: Well, he will be soon.

Joan: What are we gonna do?

Matt: Let's split. (*He starts for the door—Right*)

Peter: Oh, no you don't. (*Going after Matt and keeping him in the room*) We're in this together.

Joan: That's right Matt. We've got to face the music. (*She sits on the bench*)

Matt: We'd never be able to pay for it—probably cost a fortune.

Peter: How can you pay for an art object? It can't be replaced....
(*The guard comes in*)

Guard: (*as he enters*) What was that...? (*He sees the broken vase*) Oh, my God. Who did it?
(*Matt and Peter both speak at the same time*)

Matt: I guess I did.

Peter: I did.

Guard: Okay now, one at a time. What happened?

Peter: Well, I picked the vase up....

Guard: (*interrupting and point to sign*) Can't you read?

Matt: And I accidentally hit his arm.

Guard: (*rather sarcastically*) And you just dropped it on the floor.

Peter: (*dejectedly*) Yeah, I guess that's right.

Guard: I should' a chased you out of here when you were making so much noise.

Joan: We'll pay for it.

Guard: Pay for it?! Do you know how much this thing cost?

Matt: No, how much?

Guard: Plenty, that's how much. And it'll probably cost me my job too.

Peter: We wouldn't want that to happen, we'll take full responsibility.

Matt: Sure.
(*Mr. Smithers, the Director of the museum, walks past the archway going to his office*)

Peter: Could we talk to someone about it?

Guard: You certainly can—(*He sees Mr. Smithers*) Oh, Mr. Smithers.

Mr. Smithers: (*comes into room*) Yes, George?—(*He sees the broken vase*) Oh my, what have we here?

Guard: Well, Mr. Smithers, these kids were roughhousing it and....

Joan: We weren't roughhousing—Oh we laughed a little at the painting in the other room, but not in here. We were....

Mr. Smithers: I laugh at that painting sometimes myself.

89

Peter: (*unbelieving almost*) You do?! Then why do you have it in here?
Mr. Smithers: It's not my museum—we have to have things to please everyone.
Matt: Yeah—I never thought of that.
Peter: About the vase. I really liked it, and I just had to see what it felt like. I read the sign, but I thought, well I would never let anything happen to it, and....well....
Mr. Smithers: You're right. Pots should be felt to be fully appreciated, but if everyone picks them up we run a tremendous risk of having things like this happen. (*Indicating broken vase on the floor*)
Matt: Can we pay for it, or what can we do?
Mr. Smithers: Perhaps you *didn't* see the sign on this side of the pedestal. (*He indicates a card on the upstage side of the pedestal*)
(*They all go over and look—Joan reads*)
Joan: "This display is on loan to the Cleveland Museum for one month. The above is a copy which is available in our museum shop for $10."
Peter: Wow! That's a relief.
Matt: (*teasing Pete, but relieved*) And you were talking about the feel of the pot, and it was a fake.
Mr. Smithers: There is a difference, but it takes an expert. When the original is returned I'll let you know, and you can come to my office and hold it—if you're careful.
Guard: (*joking*) But you'll go in there *one* at a time.

CURTAIN

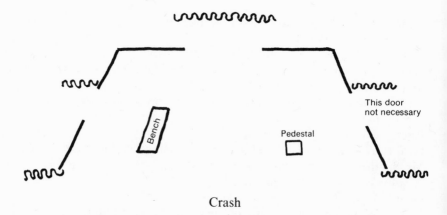

Crash

GARAGE SALE. The language used in this play is very informal, the type used within the family and its friends. There is some teasing and the closing situation is added comic effect, more than likely in a real situation Mr. Smith would return the fly and get his money back. In playing *Garage Sale* the opening needs the urgency of something about to happen. Once Mr. Smith enters, that urgency subsides since the sale has begun.

GARAGE SALE

Richard Via

CAST

Pat	the daughter
F.S.	foreign student (male or female)
George	the son
Mom, Ma	
Mr. Smith	a neighbor
Mrs. Green	a neighbor
Dad	

Garage sales are very common in the United States now. They are also known as yard sales, porch sales, lanai sales and patio sales. Sometimes several families have a joint sale, or a group will have a sale to benefit a charity. They serve many purposes besides cleaning out unwanted items and making money. They also serve as a minor social event, a chance for new neighbors to get acquainted, and a place to pick up needed items inexpensively.

SETTING: Takes place in the garage of the Burns' home. There are a couple of makeshift tables with a collection of things on them.

NOTE: "Things" sold at garage sales can be almost anything—furniture, books, toys, dishes, magazines—anything your students can bring in.

Place some things on the stage floor near the front of the stage and have the tables and big items upstage and on the sides.

Throughout the play the family can be arranging and pricing items. Mr. Smith and Mrs. Green can move about examining the various things for sale.

AT RISE: Pat is busily putting prices on bits of paper and pinning or attaching them to various articles. F.S. enters carrying a box of things to be added to the sale.

Pat: (*looking up*) Just put it down anywhere—we'll arrange it later, okay?

F.S.:   Okay. (*F.S. puts the box on the floor and begins to remove items to a table*)

Pat: Was there much more stuff?

F.S.:   Quite a bit—want me to go and get it?

Pat: Relax. Let the others bring it. You've done your share.

F.S.:   How often do you do this . . . . (*He can't think what to call it*) . . . . this . . . .

Pat: Garage sale?

F.S.:   Yeah. Garage sale.

Pat: Oh, this is the first time for us, but people are always having them.

George: (*enters with both arms full*) Here's some more junk.

Pat: (*indicating a place*) Put it over there and we'll set it up in a minute.

F.S.:   Is it really junk?

George: (*as he takes things out and places them about*) Nah, it's just stuff we don't need or use anymore.

F.S.:   So why don't you just throw it out?

Pat: That would be a waste—some of it's good.

George: Yeah—its a kinda recycling.

Pat: Ya know we got a lot of it at swap meets ourselves.

F.S.:   Swap meets?

George: You don't know about Swap Meets either?

F.S.:   No.

George: Well, its like a big garage sale, lots of people bring their stuff to a drive-in movie and sell or sometimes exchange, that's why they're called swap meets.

F.S.:   They sell at the movie?

George: No, during the day when they can't show the movie. Usually on Saturday and Sunday mornings.

F.S.:   Oh.

Ma: (*Ma enters*) You kids all set?

Pat: Not yet, but we're getting there.

Ma: Well, you'd better get moving—you know we said 10 to 3 and its almost 10.

(*Ma goes to a table and looks over the things for sale*)

George: Really? (*looks at watch*) My gosh it is!

Ma: And just what is this?! (*picking up a book*)

Pat: I don't know.

Ma: I'll tell you what it is—Its my latest book club selection—that's what it is.

Pat: Well it was with that stuff you set out.

Ma: You must've picked it up by mistake. I'd better check over everything out here. (*She starts to check carefully*)

Smith: Good morning. Store open?

F.S.: Oh, good morning Mr. Smith you're the first customer.

Smith: Do I get a special discount?

Ma: Everything's special discount, but don't buy anything until I finish checking—I just found this (*showing book*) out here.

Smith: (*to F.S.*) You're going to be a clerk?

F.S.: I suppose so—it will be good experience.

Smith: Well I'll just look around and see if I find anything I'd like. (*Smith moves about garage looking at sale items*)

George: Pat, what should I put on these paperbacks? (*holding up a book or two*)

Pat: Ten cents each—six for fifty cents.

George: And the comic books? (*George begins to put price tags on books*)

Pat: Oh, five cents.

Ma: Give them away—I want them out of the house.

Pat: Mom, is one dollar okay for this sweater?

Ma: (*Mother takes sweater and inspects it*) Mark it one dollar but you can come down to 75¢.

F.S.: I didn't know Americans would buy used clothes.

George: Sure its the in thing. Like I said recycling.

Pat: Its mostly high school and university kids—sometimes others. (*Mrs. Green enters*)

Mrs. G.: Well, what are you throwing out?

Ma: Oh, good morning Ellen, isn't it awful—look at all this stuff we had in the house we didn't use.

Mrs. G.: I'm sure if I dug around in all the closets, the attic, and the basement I'd have two garages full.

George: (*rather disappointed*) So we can't sell you anything.

Mrs. G.: Not on your life! I just came over to see what folks will buy. (*Mrs. G. starts to look about—picking up something every now and then to examine it*)

Pat: I hope other folks show up, I don't want to lug all this stuff back in the house.

F.S.: (*looks at watch*) Its only ten minutes after ten—you just started.

Smith: How much is this fly?

George: That's a dollar and a quarter.

Smith: Too much—give you seventy-five cents.

George: Settle for a dollar?

Smith: Its robbery, but okay.

Ma: Where's your father?

George: He's still reading the paper.

Pat: He said he wasn't going to get involved.

Ma: He doesn't have to get involved, but he could come out and be sociable.

F.S.: (*starts for the house*) Want me to go and get him.

Ma: That's all right I'm going in in a minute to get some bags, so I'll send him out.

Mrs. G.: (*holding them up*) Are these salt and pepper shakers?

George: I don't know, never saw them before. Are they Pat?

Pat: What?

Mrs. G.: What are these?

Pat: Salt and peppers I think.

Mrs. G.: Well now they're just real sweet. How much are they?

Pat: Isn't there a tag?

Mrs. G.: I don't see one—oh here it is on the table. . . .guess it fell off.

Ma: (*teasing*) Thought you were just looking.

Mrs. G.: That was my intention, but I just don't have much willpower —especially when it comes to salt and peppers. You know, for my collection.

Dad: (*Dad enters*) Well how's business? I expected to see the whole neighborhood here at 10 A.M. sharp.

George: It's only quarter past.

Pat: We've made two sales, that's not bad.

Ma: I'm glad you decided to join us.

Dad: It's my day off—I'll do as I please.

Ma: I wish I had a day off.

Dad: No liberation lectures during sale hours please.

Smith: Quite a load of junk ya got here Fred.

Dad: What bugs me is that I paid for all this stuff that now we don't want.

Smith: (*to George*) Guess I'll be moving on—don't see anything else I want. (*Takes out wallet*) Can you change five? (*Hands him five dollar bill*)

George: Not yet. Dad you got change for five.

Dad: Sure have if you were able to separate Smitty from some of his money. (*to Smith*) What did you buy?

Smith: A fly.

Dad: A fly? There shouldn't have been any flies for sale.

George: Sure Dad, Mom brought it down last night and put it with the stuff.

GARAGE SALE

Dad: Which fly?—let me see. (*Smith shows it to him*)

Dad: You bought that....how much!?

George: A dollar—pretty good huh?

Dad: I just bought that fly last week for ten dollars and fifty cents!

Smith: That's too bad Fred. I tell you what I'll do—I'll let you have it back for five.

CURTAIN

Vocabulary

lanai—porch (used in warmer areas of the U.S., especially Hawaii)

drive-in movie—an outdoor movie where people remain in the cars to view the film

fly—fishing lure

salt & peppers—salt & pepper shakers

bugs—bothers

THE SET UP is a simple mystery play that allows the actors to create many emotions—anger, annoyance, fear, suspicion, joy, love, and others. The creation of these will make the play interesting both for the actor and for the viewer.

THE SET UP

Richard Via

CAST

Customs Inspector
Roy Tibbs
Mr. Parker
Mrs. Parker
Ruth
Paul
Mr. Harris
Mrs. Harris
Extras

SETTING: Customs Inspection area at an airport. The baggage arrival area is on stage right. The inspection area down left center, other inspection areas and the exit are off stage up left.

TIME: Probably late afternoon.

AT RISE: We see Mr. and Mrs. Parker and Ruth Harris waiting on stage right. The Parkers are middle-aged, and Ruth is a university student, they are waiting for their suitcases to be brought from the plane.

Everyone is a little tired, but eager to meet friends and family. The customs inspector (C.I.) is pleasant, but goes about his job in a business-like manner as he checks the bags of a couple. He runs his hand quickly through the contents not upsetting anything. He closes the bag and puts a "passed" sticker on it. Roy Tibbs moves into position. The C.I. looks in and asks him a question or two which the audience cannot hear. The bag is closed and a sticker put on. Roy Tibbs moves out. The dialogue of the Parkers should start at the time Tibbs opens his bag.

Obviously the Parkers and Ruth have been waiting for some time.

Mr. Parker: (*annoyed*) Wouldn't you know, the first off the plane and the last to get our bags?

Mrs. Parker: (*trying to calm him*) We haven't been waiting so long. Don't upset yourself.

Mr. Parker: (*looking about, indicating the almost empty room*) Not long? Almost everyone has gone and we're still waiting.

Mrs. Parker: (*in order to end this discussion*) (*To Ruth*) Your bag's not here either?

Ruth: No. I thought I saw it twice, but you know so many bags are alike.

Mrs. Parker: (*glad to get into conversation*) Oh, I know. It's just terrible. So many people are traveling now, and all the bags are alike. That's why I had Jim put some wide plastic tape on ours so we could spot them right off.

Mr. Parker: The way it's going we won't have to worry. They will be the only ones left.

Ruth: The next time I travel I'm certainly going to mark mine. There was such confusion in Amsterdam. I've learned my lesson.

Mrs. Parker: (*to give him something to do*). Jim, did you pick up your tax-free package?

Mr. Parker: (*annoyed*) It's right there. (*Points beside her*)

Mrs. Parker: Oh. That's good.
(*She notices that Ruth does not have a tax-free parcel*) Why don't you pick up yours while you're waiting?

Ruth: I don't have one. I didn't buy anything.

Mr. Parker: (*unbelievable*) You didn't. Oh, I wish I'd known that. You could have picked up some stuff for me.

Mrs. Parker: (*mildly shocked*) Oh Jim, you wouldn't.

Mr. Parker: Wouldn't I?! I certainly would. Do you realize the savings? (*To Ruth*) I thought everyone bought at tax-free. Why didn't you?

Ruth: (*a little embarrassed*) Well I really went to see Europe—not to shop—and frankly, I saved the money for the trip myself, and I ran out.

Mrs. Parker: Oh. (*The bags arrive*)

Ruth: (*relieved*) Here they are. Well mine anyway. Are those two yours?

Mrs. Parker: Certainly are.... see those stripes?
(*Ruth takes her bag to the customs counter and sets it down. Mr. Parker begins to struggle with the two bags that have plastic strips on them*)

C.I.: This is all you have?

Ruth: Yes sir.

C.I.: (*mild surprise*) No duty-free package?

Ruth: No sir.

C.I.: (*matter of factly*) Would you open it please?

THE SET UP

Ruth: Just a moment.
(*The Customs Inspector, to be helpful, releases one of the latches as Ruth is trying to fit a key into the other. The Parkers are now in line behind Ruth*) Oh my, I guess I forgot to lock it. That was stupid, wasn't it?
C.I.:   Not much chance of anyone getting at it once you check in. Do you have anything to declare?
Ruth: (*As she unlatches the other lock and spreads the suitcase opens*) Only some handkerchiefs from Ireland and a leather wallet from Italy. (*She is looking at the C.I.; he is looking in the bag.*)
C.I.:   Where did you go?
Ruth: (*happily remembering*) Oh, Ireland, England, Netherlands, France, Switzerland and Italy.
C.I.:   (*teasing*) In two weeks?
Ruth: Not quite that fast. Three.
C.I.:   (*suddenly serious*) I see, and where did you get these?
(*He holds up a small box filled with cut jewels*)
Ruth: My goodness! I don't know. I never saw them before. Someone must have put them in there.
C.I.:   (*firmly*) Miss, you will save yourself a lot of trouble if you just tell me everything.
Ruth: Honestly, I never saw them before. I can't imagine—(*She turns to Mr. and Mrs. Parker in desperation*) You know me—we've been on part of the trip together. Tell him I wouldn't smuggle anything.
Mrs. Parker: (*trying to help her*) Officer, I'm sure there is some mistake.
Mr. Parker: (*firmly*) Bea, don't get involved. She may be innocent, but smugglers are good actors.
Ruth: (*turning from one to the other*) Please! I haven't done anything.
Mrs. Parker: (*more cautious*) (*To C.I.*) Of course we haven't known her long, but she seems such a nice girl.
Mr. Parker: (*warning his wife*) Bea—!
C.I.:   And what about this? (*He holds up a plastic bag filled with what could be heroin. He opens it and smells*) Yep, just as I thought. (*He puts the box and plastic bag on the table*)
Ruth: This is like some terrible dream. Everything was so wonderful until now.
C.I.:   (*takes out pad and pen*) O.K. Miss—who are your contacts? You couldn't be handling this all by yourself.
Ruth: (*in tears*) I don't know anything about it. (*Pleading with the Parkers*) Honestly, I don't.
C.I.:   It will be a lot easier on you if you give us the names of your connections.
Ruth: I don't have any connections. Why don't you believe me?

101

THE SET UP

(*She suddenly really looks into the bag for the first time and begins to search*)

All I brought in were some handkerchiefs—(*sudden realization*)—this isn't by bag. These aren't my clothes.

C.I.: Don't pull that, lady. That's the oldest stunt in the book.

Ruth: No. I mean it. It's not my bag. These aren't my clothes. I never saw any of these things before in my life.

C.I.: O.K. If you want to play the little game. (*to Mr. and Mrs. Parker*) You folks better go in there to be checked out. (*He indicates up left*) We're going to be here quite a while. (*Mr. Parker is glad to leave. Mrs. Parker lingers a moment hoping to help Ruth, but Mr. Parker beckons her away*)

Ruth: (*still searching*) If it's my bag, where are those handkerchiefs and the wallet? They're not here!

C.I.: (*sarcastic*) Handkerchiefs and wallet. There are no handkerchiefs and wallet. You were hoping I'd let sweet little you pass right on by.

Ruth: (*showing courage*) Stop it! You've got to believe me. My parents are outside. Let me get them. (*She starts to go, but he stops her*)

C.I.: You're not going anywhere. Not right now, you're not.

Ruth: (*relaxing a bit; sits on counter*) I don't know how this happened. I really don't, and this is not my bag.

C.I.: Can you prove it?

Ruth: Well, they're not my clothes. I had all casual clothes—these are too dressy. (*She picks up a dress. Obviously not the right size for Ruth, and definitely not Ruth's style*)

C.I.: (*easing up*) No, I really can't imagine you in that. But how do I know?

Ruth: (*she throws the dress back*) Oh, I just remembered something. One corner of my suitcase got dented when my father closed the car trunk on it—when he was packing to take me to the airport. (*While she is telling this she closes the suitcase to check the top corner*) See! No dents!

C.I.: You say your folks are waiting for you outside?

Ruth: Yes sir. I'm sure they are. They said they'd meet me.

C.I.: (*calls off to an officer*) Hey Paul!

Paul: (*off*) Yeah? (*He enters down left*)

C.I.: Go outside and see if a Mr. and Mrs.—

Ruth: Harris—*Joe* Harris.

C.I.: Mr. and Mrs. Joe Harris are outside.

Paul: Sure. (*He starts to go, then stops*) If so, what do you want me to tell them?

C.I.: Don't tell them anything—just bring them in.

102

THE SET UP

Paul: O.K.

Ruth: Thank you.

C.I.: That's okay—but I'm still not completely convinced.

Ruth: They'll think something's happened to me. It will scare them to death.

C.I.: Relax. And something *has* happened to you.

Ruth: It's all so unbelievable.
(*slightly amused*)

C.I.: You've said that about ten times. I don't believe a real crook could keep it up so long.

Ruth: I'm glad you're beginning to believe me.

C.I.: Where is Paul? (*He looks off left for him*) Shouldn't take him this long. There are not many people out there now.

Ruth: I planned such a scene for the moment I walked out, and now they're going to "walk in" instead.

C.I.: (*looking off left*) Well, there's Paul. He's sneaking up behind some guy. He's thrown him to the ground! Is that your Dad?

Ruth: What! Oh, my! (*She looks off left*)

C.I.: Paul's a lughead. He must have thought your Dad was an accomplice.

Ruth: That's not my Dad. (*pointing*) He's over there with Mom. They're coming in here.

C.I.: I wonder what Paul's up to. That guy really hit the dirt. Sometimes Paul takes his work a little too seriously.
(*Mr. and Mrs. Harris enter from up left. Everyone speaks at about the same time*)

Mrs. Harris: Ruth!

Ruth: Mom! Dad! Am I glad to see you.

Mr. Harris: Ruth, are you all right.
(*They embrace*)

Ruth: Yeah, I'm okay—but there's been a terrible mix-up.

Mrs. Harris: Well, we were waiting out there and this man came out with a suitcase just like yours and I said to Daddy—
(*Roy Tibbs and Paul enter up left, Paul has Tibbs firmly by the arm and carries a suitcase identical to the one on the counter*)

Mr. Harris: Here he is, and I know that's your suitcase.

C.I.: Well, I see you found the Harrises, but who's your friend?

Paul: Don't you recognize him? Look carefully.

C.I.: Oh, yeah—Tibbs!

Paul: That's right, Roy Tibbs, without a moustache.

Ruth: (*looking at new suitcase*) (*triumphant*) See—see the dent in the upper corner? *That's* my bag.

103

THE SET UP

Mr. Harris: It certainly is, honey. I hated to send you off with your new suitcase dented. When mother saw Tibbs with your bag, well, I figured something was up

C.I.: O.K. Tibbs, what have you got to say for yourself?

Roy: Tell him to let go of my arm. He's stopped the blood circulation.

C.I.: If this is your bag, Tibbs, (*pointing to the one on the counter*) *you're* going to be out of circulation for a long time.

Ruth: But how did he happen to have a bag just like mine?

Paul: It wasn't an accident. He probably watched your group leave three weeks ago. Then he bought a bag just like yours—and went to France for his haul.

Mr. Harris: Now I see. He was hoping Ruth's bag or the bag Ruth was carrying, wouldn't be inspected.

Paul: That's right. He deliberately chose Ruth for she looked so naive and honest.

C.I.: All he had to do was pick up Ruth's bag, get passed, then pretend to realize the "mistake" when she got out, and make the exchange. Then he'd have made a fortune.

Paul: It was a good plan except for a few flaws. They never think of everything.

Mr. Harris: He didn't know that Mrs. Harris and I would recognize Ruth's bag.

C.I.: Or that now-a-days we are inspecting all bags very carefully.

Mrs. Harris: Well, did you inspect the bag he was carrying?

C.I.: Certainly!

Mrs. Harris: Didn't you think it odd that he had all girl's clothes in it?

C.I.: As a matter of fact, I did comment about it. We don't really unpack you know. And he said they belonged to his wife, that she had taken ill and flew back ahead of him.

Mr. Harris: How did he open Ruth's bag if it was locked?

C.I.: To someone like Tibbs, it's no problem at all. He could open it with a fingernail file.

Roy: (*defeated and bitter to Mr. Harris*) I had everything planned. Then you screwed it up.

Paul: He didn't screw up Tibbs—you did. Joe (*the C.I.*) found the stuff. Where you screwed up was hanging around. You couldn't stand to see so much loot go down the drain. You hung around just hoping you'd get your hands on it somehow.

Ruth: But how did Paul know Tibbs had my bag?

Mr. Harris: I tipped him off when he paged us.

Paul: And the minute I saw him I recognized him. Come along, "Mr." Tibbs. (*They exit up left*)

C.I.: Well, you got a little more than you bargained for on this trip, didn't you?

Ruth: I sure did—and you really had me scared.

C.I.: I'm sorry. But when we find something like that we crack down. We can't afford to take chances.

Ruth: May we go now? I'm exhausted.

C.I.: Sure.

Paul: Thanks for the tip off.

Mr. Harris: Thank *you*.

C.I.: Oh, by the way, I hope you like the linen handkerchiefs and leather wallet.

(*Next two lines spoken together*)

Mr. Harris: What?

Mrs. Harris: I beg your pardon?

Ruth: (*happy but a little disappointed the surprise is out*) It was supposed to be a surprise.

As they exit—

CURTAIN

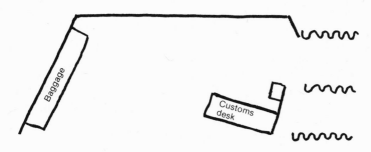

The Set Up

DON'T CALL US is a message play—its theme is women's liberation. Remember a theme cannot be acted. Since this play has very little movement, it will be necessary to make the conversation very alive to show the conflict in order to make it interesting. Little moves, such as: standing or sitting to make a point or to show dejection, a step into the group to make a strong point, can add interest to the play. Try to show different personalities for each of the characters. Rely upon your own feelings to express the ideas of the play.

DON'T CALL US

Richard Via

CAST

Females	Barb
	Judy
	Nancy
	Karen
Males	Kelly
	Joey
	Fred
	David

SETTING: A classroom or other meeting place of students such as a lounge, school lunchroom, or soda fountain.

TIME: Monday afternoon, after classes.

AT RISE: Four female students are just completing a discussion. Barb is sitting on a desk and Nancy stands beside her. Judy is seated close by, but Karen is a little removed perhaps one desk away.

Barb: Okay, then we all agree?

Judy: Sure, I'm with you.

Barb: And no matter what they say—or do?

Nancy: Absolutely.

   (*short pause—Everyone looks at Karen*)

Barb: What about you Karen?

Karen: (*hesitating*) Yeah, I think so.

Judy: Think so! This is *no* time to *think*—we've got to be sure.

Nancy: Right.

Barb: We don't want any weak sisters in this, so decide.

Karen: Of course I think you're right, but don't you think we ought to go at it gradually.

Nancy: Gradually?! If you're going to change—*change*!

Barb: You can't beat around the bush.

Judy: So what do you say?

Nancy: (*looking at watch*) What time were they supposed to be here?

Barb: Four.

Judy: What time is it now?

Nancy: Four.

Barb: (*explaining to Karen*) See. That's an example of the way they treat us.

Karen: Maybe their watches are slow, or Nancy maybe yours is fast.

Nancy: (*sitting down in disgust*) Karen will you stop? Don't find excuses for them.

Karen: Suppose they don't come at all. Then what do we do?

Barb: Will you listen to her? Karen how did you ever get mixed up with us?

Judy: Use your head. Think.

Karen: You just said don't think.

Nancy: Look, Karen maybe you ought to join us later. I don't think you're ready.

Barb: Yeah, you're likely to screw up the whole thing.

Karen: No, I won't. I'm with you. It's just that I think we ought to be rational. We shouldn't jump off the deep end.

Judy: If we don't jump off the deep end, we'll always be in the kiddie pool.

(*Suddenly the door bursts open and Kelly, Joey, Fred and David enter. They are about the same ages as the females and are full of laughter*)

Kelly: Well, here we are.

Joey: Yeah, what's up?

(*The females are a little nervous and take a moment to compose themselves*)

David: (*as he goes to Karen*) Come on. What gives?

Fred: (*looking right in her face—hoping to relax her*) You look so serious. Is something wrong?

Barb: Yes. Something is wrong.

Kelly: What?

David: (*a little worried*) Yeah, what's the matter?

Nancy: You'll find out. Just relax.

Fred: Relax! How can we relax if something's wrong?

Judy: Something's wrong and we intend to make it right.

Joey: (*relaxing*) Oh you're kidding us. Come on, what's up?

Barb: Equality.

Kelly: What?

Nancy: Equality—we demand equality.

David: Oh my gosh.

(*All the males start to laugh—David and Fred start to leave*) Women's Lib!

Barb: (*with strength to stop the boys*) That's right Women's Lib.

Fred: (*reassuring them*) You've got equality. We're all the same in this school.

David: (*annoyed with himself for being worried*) Yeah, what are you complaining about? We all get the same treatment.

Judy: We do not and you know it.

Joey: So give. What's your complaint?

Barb: We'll begin when you sit down and listen. We're dead serious— not just trying to get noticed.

Kelly: (*condescending*) Okay, fellows sit down and let the little ladies blow off their steam.

(*The boys all sit*)

Nancy: That's what we mean. You're belittling us, treating us as inferiors.

Kelly: How?

Nancy: What you just said, "Let the little ladies blow off steam." It was condescending.

David: He meant it to be friendly.

Judy: He was patronizing.

Kelly: (*admitting*) Okay I was patronizing. I won't do it again.

Fred: What are your beefs?

Barb: We won't go into those yet. We want your help.

Joey: How?

Nancy: We want you to join us.

David: Oh come off it—a bunch of guys join a woman's lib movement?

Karen: See, I told you we were rushing it.

Barb: Be quiet Karen!

Kelly: (*almost laughing*) Did you think we would join you—really?!

Fred: We'd be laughed out of school.

Judy: Why?

Joey: Being ordered around by a bunch of girls.

Nancy: There you see. You're saying that we're not capable of being leaders.

David: (*trying to get out of it*) We're not saying that. It's just . . . .

Barb: Then what are you saying? We can be leaders too, you know.

Kelly: Sure you can, we're not saying you can't. Lots of clubs have girl presidents.

Nancy: (*forcing an answer*) Which ones? Name them.

(*A slight pause—she lists the obvious and unimportant clubs*) I'll tell you which ones—the Latin club, the Home Ec. club, the Art club and the Red Cross.

Fred: So, I don't see why you're complaining.

Judy: (*demanding*) Why can't a female be president of the student body?

Nancy: (*backing her up*) Why does it always have to be a guy?

Joey: (*trapped*) There's no rule. It's just that.... (*He cannot think of a good reason*) well, it's always been a guy.

Karen: (*suddenly "with it"*) So you think it ought to always stay that way?

Barb: (*pleased*) Why Karen!

Karen: You always want a female to be the secretary, or the treasurer, or any job that does all the work and gets none of the glory.

Nancy: (*to Karen, very happy*) You've got the message.

Karen: (*rising and continuing her fire*) Why can't we be president of a sports club, or the band or the drama club?

Kelly: Why should a girl be president of a sports club. Girls' sports don't draw anyone.

Judy: (*getting angry*) Why?! Why?

Joey: What do you mean "why"?

Barb: Because all of the money goes into football and baseball. That's "why." They've never pushed female sports.

David: (*rationally*) There's no point in pushing girls' sports.

Fred: Yeah, nobody would come to see girls' sports.

Karen: Now just a minute. What about the way people turned out for Carolyn's Olympic tryout.

Judy: That's right. The only person from this school to ever have an Olympic tryout—a female.

Karen: And she had to do all her practice and tryouts at the YWCA pool because we got a new football stadium instead of a new gym, with a pool.

Judy: (*deriding them*) Okay "BOYS," now explain that.

Fred: Now who's being condescending?

Karen: It's about time. (*meaning time to be condescending*) Now you know what it's like.

Kelly: Okay let's everyone take it easy. You've made your point. What do you want?

David: They said they wanted us to join.

Barb: That's right.

Joey: How? I mean what would we have to do?

Nancy: I have charge of a discussion group on Friday and I want to bring up some of the inequalities that exist here.

Fred: Oh, you want us to promise not to hassle you?

Karen: That's right and—

Kelly: And what?

Nancy: We want you on the stage with us.

(*The males are upset by this and all talk at once*)

Fred: What!

Kelly: Are you crazy?

David: You must be kidding!

Joey: Cut the comedy.

Barb: That's right. (*a reply to Nancy's line*) *And* one of you to give a speech supporting us.

Kelly: Oh, come on! (*meaning don't be foolish*)

Judy: The guys would listen to you. It would give us strength.

David: (*teasing*) Sure they would. But you wouldn't like what we'd probably say.

Barb: You mean you're not going to do it?

Joey: How can we? Everyone would think we were a bunch of freaks.

Karen: They would not. They would think you were with the times and courageous.

Nancy: (*losing patience*) You are a bunch of freaks—you're too clannish. You're so afraid of what others will think.

Barb: Well, let me tell you we can be clannish too.

Fred: (*annoyed*) You've always been clannish—little groups of giggling prima donnas.

Karen: Oh, I admit we seemed to be like that, but whenever a guy called or gave us the high sign we dropped everything and ran.

Nancy: But no more!

Kelly: What do you mean?

Judy: From now on, *we* make the decisions. *We* decide on things.

Joey: What things?

Barb: Everything.

Nancy: Like dates, for instance.

David: (*surprised*) Dates?

Karen: That's right *dates*. Don't call us. We'll call you.

Kelly: Oh, come off it. You must be kidding.

Judy: We've been pretty foolish sitting by the phone waiting for you to call, or hoping you'd ask us for a date.

Barb: Oh, it was agony sometimes, but now the shoe's on the other foot.

Judy: Now, you can wait.

Fred: Not me.

Karen: (*sitting relaxed and sure of herself*) And we'll decide where to go, and it won't be to football games. I hate football. I like weepy movies and I intend to see them.

Kelly: Oh brother—you really are mixed up.

Joey: And you expect us to pay for this.

Nancy: Who said we were asking you to pay. We get allowances too, you know. None of you guys have part time jobs, but all of us baby sit or do something. We have money.

David: But I suppose you'll still want us to pick you up and take you home?

Barb: All of our families have cars and all of us drive.

Judy: And if you'll look at the record, the females got better grades in driving than the males.

Karen: *And* statistics prove that women are better drivers—so we'll do the picking up.

Barb: So sit by the door. You'll hear us honk.

Judy: Well, I guess the meeting's over guys. You can go home now and wait for *us* to call.

(*The boys are really puzzled. The females move away in a little group with their backs to the males*)

Kelly: (*worried*) Man, they really are mixed up.

David: Do you think they're serious or are they pulling our legs?

Joey: I think they're serious.

Fred: When do they plan to start this nonsense?

Kelly: I guess right away. Why?

Fred: What about the Prom on Saturday?

David: (*sudden realization*) Oh my gosh—that's right.

Kelly: It's what we get for getting tied down.

Joey: But they've already accepted.

David: (*disgusted*) And I've already ordered flowers—paid for them, too.

Kelly: (*trying to find hope*) They wouldn't miss the Prom. Maybe by Saturday they'll be over this kick.

(*The females all turn to the males. They have not been listening to them, but have also been discussing the dance*)

Barb: (*sweetly*) Oh about the Prom on Saturday.

Joey: (*to the boys*) See—it's going to be okay.

David: (*replying to Joey*) Yeah.

Nancy: (*very firm*) Forget it. (*this is referring to the dance and is a continuation of Barb's line. The females all turn back*)

Kelly: (*pleading*) But Barb—

Joey: (*begging*) Judy you already said okay.

David: (*enticing*) Karen I've ordered flowers.

Fred: (*angry*) You're not being fair, Nancy.

Barb: (*belittling*) Why don't you go as a group, "THE MEN"?

112

DON'T CALL US

Nancy: We're going together.

Kelly: (*hopefully*) Can we meet there? I mean, you'll still be our dates when we get there and you'll dance with us?

Karen: I doubt it. We have been dancing together for years, out of necessity. Well, now you men can start dancing together.

(*The males all look at each other and realize they don't want to dance together. They are now very unhappy*)

Barb: If you change your minds, don't *call* us, just be on stage Friday.

Nancy: And if you do a good job, wait by your phones Friday night— maybe we'll call.

(*The females start to leave. The boys sit dejectedly as the curtain falls*)

CURTAIN

Vocabulary

to screw up—ruin
jump off the deep end—to be too extreme
so give—tell, speak up
dead serious—very serious
blow off their steam—to tell what's bothering them
beefs—complaints
hassle—tease, laugh, deride
honk—to honk the car horn
cut the comedy—don't be funny
high sign—a signal
come off it—stop teasing
the shoe's on the other foot—the situation is reversed
pulling our legs—teasing us
getting tied down—dating just one person
over this kick—given up this idea
beat around the bush—hesitate
in the kiddie pool—meaning we will always be unimportant—if we don't swim
  in deep water we must stay in the children's pool.
pushed—emphasized
go at it—begin

THE SHOW MUST GO ON is a farce. It is not likely that all of the things that happen would occur, but they could. All of the people in the play are nervous, but each is showing it in a different way. Humor will be attained by playing it honestly, and not trying to be funny. When actors laugh at themselves on stage it ceases to amuse the audience. Pacing is important in a farce. Therefore it must move rapidly enough that the audience will accept what is happening. With rewriting the play may be performed by an all-male or all-female cast.

THE SHOW MUST GO ON

Richard Via

CAST

Mr. Gage	the teacher director
Bob	student
Joe	student
Helen	student
Frank	student, stage manager
Linda	student

SETTING: The action takes place in the dressing room of an auditorium. A classroom may serve as the dressing room. There is a table on stage right with makeup mirrors and makeup. Two chairs are in front of the table. Another table and chair are along the up center wall. A single chair is down stage left. There is a door in the center of the left wall and another on the right of the rear wall.

TIME: About 7:45 P.M.

AT RISE: Mr. Gage is talking to the students giving them last minute directions. He stands up left center. Helen is seated in the chair down right. Joe is seated next to her perhaps straddling his chair. Bob is in a chair upstage and Linda is in the chair down left.

Gage: Okay kids, I guess that takes care of everything. Just remember they're your friends and families out there in the audience. They're rooting for you. And remember to speak up. The first duty of an actor is to be heard, and don't rush your first lines. Let the audience "tune in" to you. So I guess that's it.

Oh yes, and pick up your cues. Is there anything else? If not, I'll go out front and get a seat and enjoy the show: So break a leg. (*Everyone laughs—he starts to exit*)

Bob: Mr. Gage, I have a question.

Gage: Yes Bob?

Bob: Why did I ever agree to be in this play? (*Everyone laughs*)

Gage: (*a little worried*) Bob you're not serious are you?

Joe: (*goes to Bob*) Stop worrying. You'll be great.

Helen: There's nothing to worry about. (*She turns back to the mirror and stares at herself*)

Joe: Relax and take a deep breath. Remember Mr. Gage always said if you're nervous take a deep, long breath. Didn't you, Mr. Gage?

Gage: That's correct.

Bob: That's a big help. I can't even take a short breath. (*rises and takes a few short gasps*)

Helen: All this talk about being nervous is making me nervous. I'm trying to concentrate on my role.

Joe: (*noticing her staring into the mirror*) Doesn't it scare you? (*She gives him a dirty look*)

Gage: Now let's not upset each other. Let's just keep our minds on the play. All right? (*He starts to leave but stops when Joe starts speaking*)

Joe: (*pacing back and forth up stage he begins to recite his lines in a loud voice*) "No Horace, I will not. I have told you several times now that the deal is closed and furthermore...."

(*Linda throws up her hands in disgust and goes to the upstage table. She picks up a box of powder and stands with her back to the audience*)

Helen: Would you *please* be quiet.

Joe: I'm working on my part. Mr. Gage said we should. (*To Mr. Gage*) Didn't you?

Gage: Yes, I did. But a little quieter perhaps Joe.

Joe: Okay. (*then in a loud stage whisper he continues*) "The deal is closed and furthermore if we ever discover that you....that you....if we ever discover that you...."

(*using his regular voice*) What is that line? (*He goes to the table left and picks up his script to look up his line*)

Frank: (*The door suddenly bursts open, which startles Mr. Gage, and Frank the stage manager puts his head in and shouts*)

Fifteen minutes! (*closes door*)

Helen: What!?

Frank: (*opens the door again*) I said "fifteen minutes." (*closes door*)

Helen: Time goes so fast. Oh, I hope I'll be ready. (*She continues to look in the mirror*)

Bob: (*suddenly bursts forth in a very loud vocal exercise*) La- la- la- la- la- la- la-

(*Linda and Helen both jump with fright at the sound. Then Linda begins to cry*)

116

THE SHOW MUST GO ON

Linda: Look! Look what you made me do! (*She turns around and we see that the whole front of her black dress is covered with white powder*)

Bob: *I* made you do? I *made* you do? I wasn't near you.

Linda: You scared me when you yelled.

Bob: I was not yelling. I was warming up my voice. It was a voice exercise.

Linda: It was yelling. Mr. Gage what am I going to do? (*Mr. Gage rushes to her and starts to brush the powder off*)

Gage: I knew something like this would happen. How many times have I told you to put on your makeup first, then put on your costume?

Linda: I know, but they kept saying I had to get dressed. I had done everything but powder. Anyway all the powder puffs were being used. (*The door bursts open again*)

Frank: Linda is this ice cream your prop?

Linda: Yes.

Frank: Don't leave it on the stage manager's desk. Here! (*holding it out to her*)

Gage: Just put it down somewhere Frank. I'm trying to get this powder off her dress. (*Frank puts the ice cream on the chair on stage left and exits*) Now go get a damp towel and rub your dress gently.

Linda: Yes, sir. (*She exits through the up right door*)

Joe: (*starts to whistle*)

Gage: Joe!

Joe: Sir?

Gage: Don't whistle in the dressing room. It's bad luck. You know that.

Joe: Sorry.

Bob: Mr. Gage would you please check my makeup? (*He turns around and he has on much too much lipstick and one eyebrow is about an inch higher than the other*)

Gage: Oh my, who did that?

Bob: I did.

Gage: Give me a tissue. We've got to get it off.

Bob: Why?

Gage: (*handing him a mirror*) Well, just look at it.

Bob: I can't see anything.

Gage: You can't?

Bob: No sir, I don't have my glasses on.

Gage: Why didn't you wear your glasses when you put on your makeup?

Bob: I did but my eyebrows come right at the top of my glasses and so I had to take them off. I did the best I could.

Gage: Would someone please hand me a tissue.

Helen: Here you are Mr. Gage (*resumes her stare*) (*Mr. Gage rubs a bit, but it won't come off*)

Gage: I'll have to use cold cream. Where is the cold cream?

Helen: It was here a moment ago.

Gage: Has anyone seen the cold cream? I've got to hurry. We only have a few minutes.

Bob: Should I go and wash it off? (*Linda comes back on stage holding a paperbag which she is twisting nervously*)

Gage: No it won't wash off. We'll have to use cold cream. Would everyone please look around you for the cold cream. (*Everyone, including Linda, begins to hunt*)

Linda: (*weakly*) I'll forget my lines.

Gage: What?

Linda: I'll forget my lines.

Gage: No you won't Linda. You're just nervous. You know your lines perfectly. Your dress looks fine, so just relax.

Linda: I can't. I don't even remember my first line.

Bob: (*No one is paying attention to him*) What about my face?

Gage: What?

Bob: My face! Nobody's doing anything.

Joe: (*trying to be funny*) What can we do? You were born with it.

Bob: (*not in the mood for joking*) Oh, that's so funny.

Gage: Now let's not start teasing each other.

Linda: (*starts to cry*) I don't remember any of them. I want to go home.

Gage: Just relax Linda. Take a deep breath. Shake your arms....and stop twisting that bag you're making *me* nervous.

Linda: I can't help it.

Gage: What's in it anyway?

Linda: I don't know.

Bob: What am *I* going to do?

Gage: It's not a prop is it? (*He opens bag and looks in*) It's the cold cream! *You were holding* it all the time. (*He takes out the jar of cold cream and starts to work on Bob*)

Linda: (*letting out a loud howl*) But I didn't know. I couldn't help it.

Gage: I didn't mean to yell, Linda. You must realize that I'm a little upset, too. Helen?

Helen: (*very calm*) Yes, Mr. Gage?

Gage: Would you talk to Linda while I fix Bob's face?

Helen: Certainly Mr. Gage. Linda? (*Goes to Linda*)

Linda: Ye-ee-ss—?

Helen: Let's go over here and run over our lines. (*They go to stage left*)

Linda: (*sniffling*) All right.

Helen: Now let's see. I'm sitting when you first enter—so I'll just sit here. (*She sits on the ice cream*)

118

Linda: (*trying to stop her*) But.... but....

(*There is a moment of silent realization*)

Helen: (*starting low then building in volume*) Oh....oh....oh....oh...
Mr. Gage!

(*Linda starts to laugh and grabs Mr. Gage's arm just as he starts to redo Bob's eyebrow*)

Gage: Don't bother me now (*but the damage is done, once again Bob has a misplaced eyebrow*) Now look!

Helen: Mr. Gage, what will I do?

Gage: Can't you see I'm busy?

Helen: But my dress!

Gage: What's wrong with it? (*Helen rises and turns so audience and Mr. Gage can see the mess on the back of her dress*)

Helen: Look!

Gage: How did you do *that*? (*The door bursts open, it's Frank*)

Frank: Everyone on stage please. (*He starts out*)

Gage: (*very determined*) Hold the curtain.

Frank: I can't. The music is almost over.

Linda: (*to Helen*) My prop! You sat on my prop. Mr. Gage what will I use.

Gage: Don't bother me. (*to Frank*) Don't take the curtain up. Do you understand?

Frank: But you always said....

Gage: Forget what I said. (*But Frank is a good stage manager and will get the curtain up on time*)

Frank: Places please. Everyone on stage. (*Joe, Bob, and Linda start to go*)

Helen: Mr. Gage, what shall I do?

Gage: (*realizing defeat*) Just don't turn your back to the audience. Walk sideways.

Helen: (*demonstrating*) Like this?

Gage: (*weakly*) Yes that's ri—(*He suddenly faints and collapses to the floor. Everyone rushes to him*)

Joe: My gosh, he's fainted.

Bob: Mr. Gage—Mr. Gage!

Helen: Oh, this is terrible. (*The door opens again. It's Frank*)

Frank: Places. Curtain going up!

Linda: But Mr. Gage has fainted!

Frank: "No matter what happens," he always said, "the show must go on." (*with new strength they all start for the "stage" as the curtain falls*)

CURTAIN

119

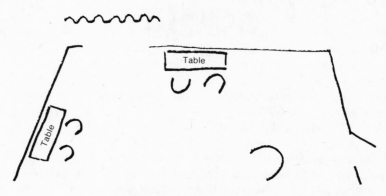

The Show Must Go On

ACT III

PRODUCTION

If you discover that your play is such a smash success in the classroom that you feel you really should let the rest of the world see it, what do you do? How do you go about transferring from a classroom production to a full production with makeup, costumes, scenery and lighting?

First let me say, "Keep it simple." Some of the most highly recommended plays, *Happy Journey*, *Long Christmas Dinner*, etc. do not require scenery or properties. Also, there is a great deal of experimental theatre that uses available light and adjusts to the room in which it plays. Young people particularly will "build" scenery in their minds, plus provide the necessary costumes and properties. What they create cannot be equalled by your limited budgets.

Still you want the full production? Okay, again I say, "Keep it simple." Many amateur productions come off poorly because they tried to do too much. I have seen plays that needed six light cues (usually "off" and "on") ruined because of numerous errors resulting from a complicated lighting plot which they did not need.

Keep it simple. Do not bite off more than you can chew on the first trial. As you develop your students' ability at production you may make your presentation more elaborate.

Your production activities should also be timed to learn English. Help your production staff to make up a special vocabulary list of the words they need to carry out their activities. You may even provide them with some suitable dialogues connected with their particular job. In this way the students who are behind the scenes will also be learning English. As an illustration, I received a program from a university drama group with this message printed in it:

Being members of the English Speaking Society we decided that everybody should use only English during the rehearsals and all.

121

It was not only for the cast but also for the staff. It was not easy at all to carry out everything in English, but gradually we got used to it. Everybody seemed to be enjoying it, not suffering too much. After all, it was a great help for us all to improve our English speaking ability. It also helped to strengthen togetherness between us.

I might add here that for the full productions of Model Productions we had as many as eighty students involved. Each production had about thirty-eight rehearsals. English was the language of communication for all of these rehearsals and for the backstage crew.

Crew members should have scripts available to them and be a part of all early rehearsals when the play is discussed. After they have started work on the production they should attend rehearsals as often as possible to be sure their work is fitting in with that of the director and actors.

BACKSTAGE

Scenery

Plan your set to fit the needs of the play and the stage you are using. If for instance your stage is very large, and the action of the play takes place

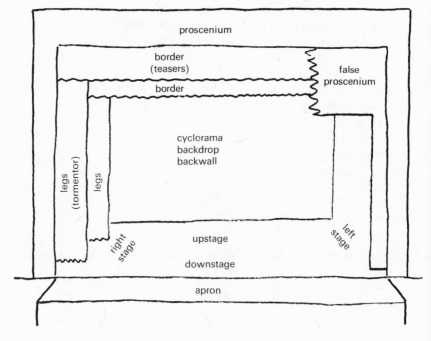

Figure 1.   Proscenium stage.

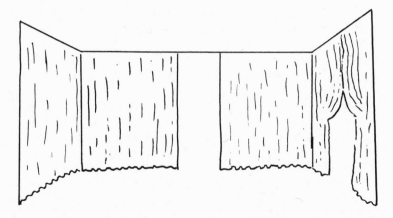

Figure 2.   Curtain set.

Figure 3.   Curtain set with door and window flats.

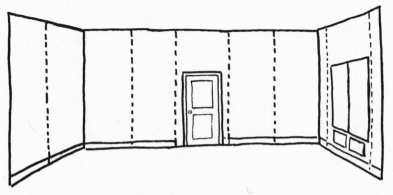

Figure 4.   Box set.

123

in a kitchen, you will need to make the proscenium opening smaller. This may be done with a false proscenium (Fig. 1) or by masking in with legs and borders.

Most of the stages you will use, hopefully, will be equipped with a set of curtains. The simplest setting might be to open the stage curtains to denote doorways and windows (Fig. 2). To make this curtain set more elaborate add door or window flats at the openings (Fig. 3). If you want to go even further, you may build a simple "box set" (Fig. 4).

It is important to remember that scenery is relatively easy to build and need not be too expensive. At the same time, however, it should be strong, easy to handle, and require little moving or storage space.

I have seen students build an entire upstage wall of a set and the front of two-story house in one piece. To them it seemed like a good idea—quicker, easier, used less lumber, and once in position most of the set was up. Neither of these sets fit the last three requirements listed above. One had to be cut in half in order to move it to the theatre, then had to be repaired and repainted once in. The other was much too top heavy and

set ¾ inch
from edge

nails or lash
line cleats

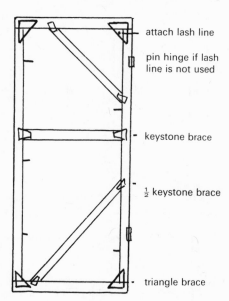

attach lash line

pin hinge if lash
line is not used

keystone brace

½ keystone brace

triangle brace

frame and center brace—1" × 3" lumber
braces—1" × 2" lumber
Triange and keystone braces may be made of
plywood. Tempered hardwood or tin may
be used.

Figure 5.   Flat.

124

considerable time was spent giving it proper support. One good thing did happen from these experiences, however, the students did learn from doing and later did excellent work using their new knowledge.

Large units of scenery do not save time, are much more difficult to make secure, very difficult to handle, and impossible to store. For these reasons it is wise to make many smaller units and fit them together. These basic units are called flats (Fig. 5). They are made of a lightweight inexpensive wood frame and covered with cloth. The size of the flats will depend on the size of your stage. I do not think they should be over 12 feet high or wider than 5 feet 9 inches. Of course, you may, and probably will need, many smaller flats. Often I have used flats that were only 8 feet high with great success.

Once you have the frame made, cover the front with cloth, usually cotton canvas or muslin. Fit the selvage along one outer edge of the frame. Tack the four corners to the frame. Do not stretch the cloth too tight as

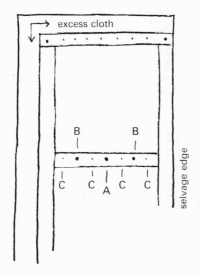

To cover flat

    place selvage edge on one side
    tack four corners
    add tacks about 6 inches apart about $\frac{1}{4}$ inch
       from edge
    on cross brace, add tack A, then tacks B,
       then tacks C
    cut excess cloth off
    glue cloth to frame

Figure 6. Covering of flat.

it will shrink when painted; however, avoid wrinkles. On the selvage side place tacks about six inches apart and about a quarter inch from the inside edge of the frame. Now, tack the other three sides, and be careful of diagonal puckers. Tack the cloth to the center support by placing one tack in the center, then one in the center of the space on either side, and again in between each tack. Once the tacks are in, the loose canvas along the edge may be glued down. Add another row of tacks all around about one foot apart and a half inch from the outer edge of the frame. Once the glue is dry you may cut off the excess cloth from the three sides of the flat (Fig. 6).

Flats that are to contain doors or windows are a little more difficult to make. Generally, it is not wise to make a special flat for windows but to make a flat with a door opening and fill in with a plug. By doing this it enables you to have extra doors if needed for another production (Fig. 7).

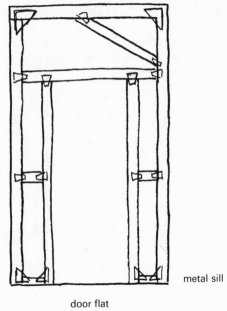

metal sill

door flat

1-inch lip added before covering with cloth

spin or turn button on back of plug to "lock" into place

Plug used in door flat to make windows.
Plugs may be used top and bottom.

Figure 7.   Door flat.

126

Regular doors will be too heavy for your set; therefore, you will need to make a door the same way you make a flat. Often it is possible to avoid doors by having onstage doorways open onto hallways, so the exterior door is not visible. Windows that are hung with very full sheer curtains, drapes, and valances will not need an actual window or plug in them.

Painting should be done with a water base paint. Check with your local stores as to the types available that would be suitable. To make your set more interesting, you may wish to experiment with a stencil to achieve a wallpaper effect. Texturing may be done by splattering one or two other colors on the painted flat. These dots of paint should not be more than a quarter inch in diameter. You may also achieve this effect by dipping a sponge in paint or crumpling up a cloth wet with paint and rolling them over the painted flat. Before doing this to your flat, be sure you experiment on a test board. Light reflecting from the other colors is different from that of the base coat thus giving the wall a texture rather than flat look. Detailed information on these techniques will be found in the books listed in the appendix.

Putting up the set is not as difficult as it may seem. If you are using pin hinges, place the flats together and insert a wire in the hinge. Then bend the wire so that the hinge is secure (Fig. 8). Using a lash line is quicker if cleats are available. If cleats are not available, a finishing nail will do. In a short time your students can learn to snap the line and lace the flats together (Fig. 9).

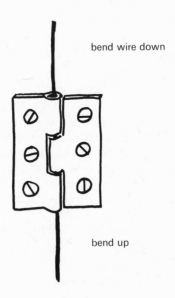

bend wire down

bend up

Figure 8.   Pin hinge to join flats.

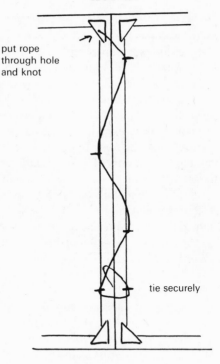

put rope
through hole
and knot

tie securely

Figure 9.   Lashing.

Flats that are joined at right angles will stand alone, flats not at right angles and doorways will need a brace for added support.

Simple and interesting sets may also be made by using cutouts or set pieces. These are flat pieces used to suggest location. They are particularly useful for exterior scenes (Fig. 10). In this set, the tree trunk can be made from a narrow flat with plywood, pasteboard or tempered hardboard added to give proper shape. The foliage is made of cloth and hung from the same pipe as the border (if another pipe is available use it) in front of the trunk. The rock is easiest made of plywood. If an actor should need to sit on the "rock" a stool could be placed behind it. The mountain shape should be made from a triangular flat with the uneven edge cut from plywood and added.

The final job of the scenery crew will be to mask in. This means to cover any back stage area that may be seen by the audience. Front curtains are pulled into mask the sides, and the borders are lowered to hide the back wall and lighting units. You may also need backing outside the doors.

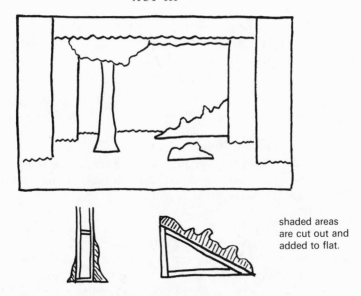

Figure 10. Cutouts or set pieces.

shaded areas
are cut out and
added to flat.

If your side doors are hinged on the upstage side of the door jamb, it may eliminate the need for masking. Often the legs of the stage curtain may be used for masking doorways. Of course, if you wish to give a more professional look, build more flats and use them as masking (Fig. 11).

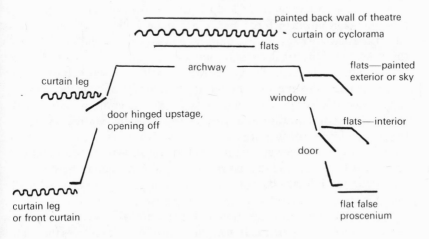

Figure 11. Masking.

129

Makeup

"An accidental touch of the makeup brush on my face served to open the flower of the role.... Every actor should have an attitude of great respect, affection and attention for his makeup."

Constantin Stanislavski
An Actor's Handbook

One of the first things an amateur thinks of when he is told he is to be involved in a play is makeup. Most of us are fascinated by the stories written about the complicated and elaborate makeups used by stage and film stars for various roles. Makeup for many represents the *theatrical* of the theatre.

Before going into the why and how of makeup there are several points I would like to make about the extra values it provides. The makeup created for (or by) the actor can help the actor solidify the oneness of self and the character. Makeup should be rehearsed and experimented with several times before dress rehearsals and performances. At these times as actors work on their faces and see the subtle changes that take place, their identity in the role will become stronger. The physical look provided by makeup will be a strengthening power. It is good to remind you here that makeup should not be used as a mask to hide behind for security. Great actors who use masks in their performance, such as the Japanese Noh actors, must create so strong a character that the mask becomes alive. This may be the height of the acting of inner feeling.

A second extra value of makeup is that it gives the actor a time to relax and concentrate before a performance. Of course, this will only be true if the actor arrives at the theatre well in advance of curtain time. In the professional theatre in the U.S., actors are required to be in the theatre at "half hour" (theoretically this means one-half hour before the curtain goes up, in actuality it is forty minutes). Working on one's makeup takes concentration which gets the mind away from the humdrum problems of the day. This concentration and attention to detail can draw the actor into the play and his identity in it.

With these two important points made about the extra values of make-up, I must hasten to add that we must not allow makeup to become too important and fall into the trap of using too much makeup. As with all of the technical aspects of the production—keep it simple.

Makeup has one main function and that is to help the actor portray his character to the audience. It does this in two ways: it replaces the color and details washed out by stage lighting, and adds character touches when needed. With the exception of stylized plays or roles, actors should never have a "madeup" look. They should look natural. If an actor looks made-up then he either has on too much on or it was applied incorrectly. Exceptions to this, of course, are if the character should look "madeup," or if the style or fashion is one that accents makeup.

As part of the makeup activities and study of makeup, have your students collect photographs from magazines, and elsewhere, of various types of faces. Study these photographs to see how light and shadow play on the face. This is especially helpful when working on an old age makeup. Also have your students observe the faces that they see about them during their various activities during the day.

There are many makeup supplies suitable for the stage at cosmetic counters almost everywhere. These include base makeup (cake and cream), eyeshadows, rouges, mascara, false lashes, eyebrow pencils and powders.

There are several types of makeup available and they each need to be handled differently. Your supplier will be able to give you any special instructions you may need. Cake makeup is applied with a moist sponge. Pan stick and soft paint (in a tube) are smoothed out with moistened fingertips. Grease paint which comes in sticks, tins, or jars needs to have a thin layer of cold cream as a first step.

Before starting on makeup be sure you are not wearing your costume. The costume should be put on after the makeup is completed. You may wish to protect your hair or clothing with towels.

If you are using grease paint, first apply a *thin* layer of cold cream over the entire area to be covered with makeup. Tissue it off leaving a very thin film. *Never* use cold cream when using a water soluble foundation. The procedure from this point is the same, except for cake makeup. Dot the face with the base or foundation color (Fig. 12). Spread evenly over

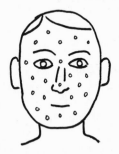

Dot base makeup on face. Smooth base evenly over face with fingertips. Be sure to blend down onto neck, back of neck, and on ears.

Figure 12.

131

the entire face, making sure to blend down the neck, on the ears and the back of the neck to avoid a harsh line where the makeup stops. A very common mistake made by beginners is that too much base is used. A heavy base melts, rubs off, absorbs lines and shadows, and worst of all, looks bad.

Place a dot or two of rouge where you wish then blend out in straight strokes rather than circular (Fig. 13). Usually rouge is placed on the high point of the cheek and blended out and up. Women's rouge should be the same color as used on the lips for a regular makeup. Men, except when wishing to give the effect of old age or a sallow complexion, should use a fairly dark red liner blended with brown liner as rouge. To blend makeup colors put a small amount of each on the side of the palm and mix with your fingertips.

Dot rouge on high point of cheek. Blend into base with fingertips. Use straight strokes rather than circular ones.
Rouge placed closer to the nose tends to make the face seem narrower, and away from the nose wider.

Figure 13.

Eye shadow goes only on the upper lid (Figs. 14 and 15). Women may use many different colors to suit their makeup or costumes. The most common are blue, green, brown, and lavender. A mixture of blue-green, blue-gray and green-gray is possible. Men should use brown or a mixture of brown and red similar to that used on the cheeks. It is most unusual for men to use green, blue or other colors. For eye lining (see Fig. 16) use an eyebrow pencil which is a wooden pencil with black or brown grease "lead."

In most cases when penciling in the eyebrow follow the natural curve (Fig. 17). To raise or lower the brow slightly draw the lines at the top or bottom of the brow. If you wish to block out the eyebrow to reposition

Eye shadow placed close to the bridge of the
nose and blended out gives the eyes a deep-set
look.
Do not blend shadow into eyebrow.

Figure 14.

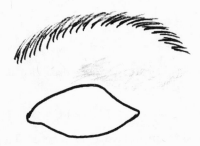

Eye shadow blended on center of lid and out
enlarges appearance of eye, and makes eyes
seem wider apart.

Figure 15.

A brown or black line, made with a brush or
lining pencil, drawn close to the lashes on the
upper lid and slightly below the lashes on the
lower lid helps accent the eyes.
The lines should not meet and should be gently
blended out with the fingertip at point A.

Figure 16.

133

it, moisten a piece of soap and rub it over the eyebrow to block it out before applying the base makeup. When it is dry apply the base and place the eyebrow where you wish. Often men with heavy eyebrows need no pencil on the brows.

A—wrong

B—right

Eyebrows should not be heavy drawn lines (A), but drawn with quick, short strokes (B). Use black or brown pencil depending upon hair color.

Figure 17.

Often Japanese students wanted a "high nose." To achieve this they put a heavy white line down the center of the nose and dark brown on either side. This made their noses look like it had a white streak down the middle and dark brown on both sides. Actually, the principle was okay, it was the application that was at fault. The highlight should be a lighter color then the base. This can be white blended into the base color that is on the nose or can be mixed separately and applied. The sides of the nose should be a slightly darker base or brown blended very carefully. No harsh line should be noticed, and the shading on the sides or the highlight should be barely discernible (Fig. 18).

Lip rouge is applied next, making the desired shape. Men should never have the look of having on lipstick, the same brown and red mixture may be used.

Using a translucent or neutral shade of powder, pat powder over the entire makeup to set it. Don't rub it on as this may smear the makeup. Take a very soft brush and brush the powder off. Moisten the fingers and clean the eyelashes, women may now add mascara or false eyelashes if they wish. If the play contains a kissing scene, then the lips should be powdered well and blotted to keep from leaving a stain. The above des-

cription is a "straight makeup"; its purpose is to make the actor look like
himself or herself.

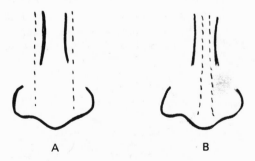

A   B

To widen nose run a wide highlight down the
center (A).

To make the nose seem narrower, shadow the
sides and have a narrow highlight down the
center (B).

In both cases, blend shadow and highlight
carefully. Avoid harsh lines.

Figure 18.

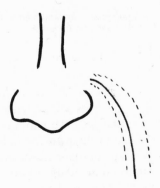

Using the crease formed when smiling as a guide,
draw a line with a pencil or brush. Soften by
blending the line out slightly with a brush or
fingertip. Add highlight on outside or both sides
of line (space that is within dotted lines).
Highlight may be applied first if desired.

Figure 19.

135

For age you will need to add wrinkles. All wrinles are basically made the same way (Figs. 19 and 20)—a line is made where you wish the wrinkle. A brown liner is probably the most useful for this, but a much darker shade of the base makeup will work. Soften the line with the fingertip or a brush to erase the harsh line. A highlight, using a lighter shade of the base may be added on one or both sides of the line. Blend carefully to achieve a natural look.

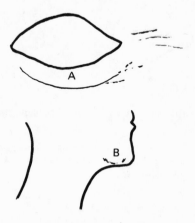

Upper: Crow's-feet and eye pouch. Highlight area A.

Lower: Sagging jowl. Highlight area B. Shadow lower part of cheek and underside of chin.

Figure 20.

When putting on an old age or middle age makeup, do not try to put on too many lines. An excess of lines will probably look like a dirty face, especially from a distance, and hide the natural expressions which are much more important. Experiment with the lines you wish to use to achieve age using Fig. 21 as an approximate maximum.

Hair styles are very important in aiding an actor to present his character. I have discovered, however, that the hair color is not important except in very special cases. I refused to allow students to add the various colored powders to try and become blonds or redheads. The colors did not go with the Japanese features or skin tones, and the powders were constantly falling on everything. Most people have dark hair. If the actor is creating properly, the hair color will not be important. The exception I made was to allow white to be added for age. Try to find silver spray, white cake makeup or white mascara. If none of these are available, white grease

136

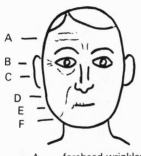

A — forehead wrinkles
B — crow's feet
C — eye pouch
D — smile crease
E — lip lines
F — jowl

Middle-age and old-age lines. Too many lines become messy and confused. Use only the vital ones.

Figure 21.

paint, white powder or white shoe polish can be used. Use all of these sparingly, probably at the temples and some streaks from the hairline.

To apply cake makeup, moisten a sponge (damp not wet) and rub over the cake and then apply to the face. Be careful that you do not streak it. If it should streak, moisten the sponge and smooth it out. A dry rouge will probably apply easier than a moist rouge. Some actors apply moist rouge directly to the skin, then apply the cake makeup over it. This will take some experimenting and practice. Lines can be drawn on with pencil, but shading and highlighting will need to be done with other shades of cake makeup. One great advantage of cake makeup is that you generally do not need to powder.

To remove cake makeup all you will need to do is wash with soap and water. For other makeup apply cold cream and spread over entire area (a wonderful mess), tissue off, and then use soap and water.

Your makeup kit should include:

Base—any type: four colors, two darker colors for men and two lighter colors for women.
Liners—blue, green, brown, black, red, white.
Pencils—black, brown.
Translucent powder
Powder puff
Soft brush
Shading brushes

Cold cream
Tissues
Mirrors
Towels

Two final notes on makeup—if you use very strong colors in lighting, it will affect the makeup. Be sure to check this before the performance. And, a beautiful makeup job never saved a poor performance, but a poor makeup job has hurt a good performance.

Properties

The biggest problem of the property staff is to locate, then obtain, suitable furniture. Your students will have to use their imaginations and ingenuity to come up with a solution, and very often you will just have to make-do.

During the war I traveled in Europe with a Broadway play. Naturally, we could not carry the necessary furniture with us. We had slip covers made to fit folding chairs which were usually available. Three chairs together served as a sofa, two a love seat and a single chair for a lounging chair. You may achieve a similar effect by draping cloth over chairs. Be sure, however, that it is pinned or tacked in such a way that it will not slip off.

Tables generally do not seem to be a problem and often wooden boxes may be painted and used.

If the furniture is not actually used, but is for decorative effect then it may be made of corrugated cardboard. Cabinets and bookcases can be made this way easily.

Hand props are those properties which are actually handled by the actors. These include such things as letters, dishes, suitcases, gifts, food, etc. The property staff should set up a table or space on either side of the stage or rehearsal area on which to place all props which actors take on stage. The props should be placed in the same place at each rehearsal or performance. Likewise, the on-stage props should be in exactly the same place so that the actor will not have to hunt for the prop or worry that it is not there.

Dressing props are those properties which are used to decorate the stage. This would include such things as pictures, flowers, books, knickknacks and some furniture. An outstanding job of dressing props was done by a student for *You Can't Take It With You.* All of the elaborate picture frames were made from cut and decorated styrofoam. It is easy to carve, glue, and paint. The pictures were copies of famous paintings from slick magazines.

Books are very often used for stage dressing. Since books are rather heavy it is a simple matter to fake them. The easiest way, of course, is to have the set crew paint them on the flats. If, however, there are real book-cases, for a realistic effect, you may make a cardboard cut-out of books and fit them into the shelves. Be sure to have "books" of varying heights as well as matched sets of "books."

Suggestions:

1. The property staff should have props or substitute props available for the actors as soon as the blocking rehearsals are completed.

2. No one should touch a prop once it is placed except the actor who uses it.

3. All actors should check their props before each rehearsal or per-formance.

4. All food and drinks that are used on stage should be kept in a sani-tary condition. Clean up all dishes immediately after the performance.

5. Generally food on stage should be easy to handle and to consume. Therefore, moist foods are better than very dry for they may be swallowed easier. Also portions should be small.

6. Do not use sharp knives or swords on stage.

7. If you borrow furniture for your production, it will be a good idea to give a good coating of paste wax furniture polish to all wooden areas to prevent minor scratches. Do not polish the furniture as the sheen will reflect the stage lights. Remove the wax before returning the furniture and return it promptly after the performance. If owners are aware that you are very careful they will be more willing to help you another time.

8. Close observation of films and the many photographs in U.S. and British magazines and catalogues will provide you with ample information about the decor of rooms.

Lighting

As with scenery, keep it simple. In your classroom you should use avai-lable light. This is also good advice in many other situations.

Often young people want to be "dramatic" and use very dim light. This probably stems from watching movies where there seems to be very little light used or from observing still photographs of stage plays which often appear dark. Actually to achieve this kind of lighting requires a great deal of lighting equipment and knowledge. The best thing an amateur lighting technician can do is to remember that the job is lighting and to put some light on stage. Harsh, overly bright light is not desirable, but it is better to have too much light than too little. Especially in the case of students who are trying to comprehend a foreign language, it is important that everyone is able to see the faces of the actors. Have you ever noticed how difficult it is to communicate properly over the phone in a foreign language (and often in your native language) because we cannot "read" the person's face? Therefore, it is important to have enough light for the audience to be aided by the facial expression and thus able to comprehend and follow the story.

White light is very harsh on actors and scenery, therefore, we usually

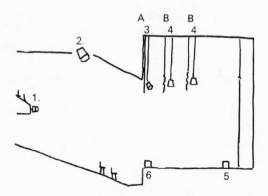

Figure 22.   Positions of stage lighting instruments.

1. Balcony or front spots
2. Beam or ceiling lights
3. Bridge or first pipe spots
4. Strip or border lights
5. Strip or ground lights
6. Footlights

A. Front curtain
B. Borders

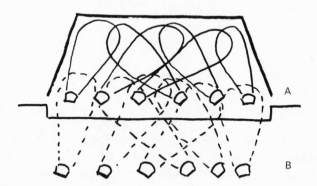

Figure 23.   Cross lighting.

A. Spotlights on the bridge or pipe
B. Front spots or balcony spots
Support lights would come from border lights.

140

use some form of color to soften this harshness. The most common material is gelatine which comes in a wide variety of colors.

In most plays you will want to use a combination of colors to achieve a natural effect. You will find it effective if you have the warm colors (pink, straw, amber, etc.) in the spots that are angled in one direction and the cool colors (lavender, pale blue, steel, etc.) angled in the opposite direction (see Figs. 22 and 23).

The mood and attention of the audience may be controlled by light. A bright stage using warm colors will impart a happy atmosphere whereas a dim stage with predominately cool colors will give a somber feeling. A high concentration of light will cause the audience to focus on that area. Even a person lighting a cigarette or candle will immediately attract the attention of the entire audience.

Some helpful hints on lighting:
1. Light the actors, not the scenery.
2. Be sure there is light in all of the areas of the stage where action takes place.
3. Use cross lighting. Rather than have lights play straight on the stage have them angled to the various areas. Lights angled help mold the actors and also cut down on the possibilities of shadows on the back wall. Strong lights from the front "flatten" the actors.
4. Avoid strong "follow spots" except in very special cases. It is rare that we want to see the "circle" of light or the shadows such a strong light cause. General stage lighting should also avoid such "circles."
5. Keep light off the apron and proscenium arch.
6. If the front curtain is a slow mechanical one it may be wise to start in a black out and begin the fade up when the curtain is about half way. The reverse would be true at the end of an act when the curtain is coming down.
7. Do not move lighting instruments during a performance when the curtain is up. The audience will be aware of light moving about the set.
8. Back and side lighting will help mold the actors and eliminate actors' shadows from the scenery.

Costumes

Since most of the plays you will be presenting will be rather new plays, the costumes will be modern dress and no problem.

In case you are performing a play that requires a period costume, it is possible to suggest the period very simply. A long skirt for example, is suitable for any period when ladies wore long skirts. If your play requires many changes of period costumes, give each actor a basic costume and let the changes be denoted with a variety of belts, aprons, scarves, shawls, sashes, etc.

Often in a script you may notice an exact description of what an actor wears. Rarely is it necessary to have an exact replica of the description, however, you will need to change any line reference to such costumes.

Hints:

1. If the costume is at all unusual or different from normal attire, the actor should rehearse in a similar costume as often as possible.

2. Costumes should be put on after makeup to avoid spilling powder or other makeup on the costume.

3. Costumes should be pressed—the stage lights will accentuate any wrinkles.

4. Costumes should be hung up after each performance.

5. White and very bright shiny fabrics should be used cautiously, unless the actor is supposed to stand out in a scene.

6. White and light colors make a person seem larger.

Sound

Often students desire background music for their plays. This probably is a result of the rather constant background music used in films and television. It is rare in the professional theatre. However, there is nothing wrong with using background music if it is handled wisely.

Hints:

1. Background music should be just that—background. This means it should come from backstage speakers and not loud enough to drown out the dialogue.

2. The audience should not be aware of the music. If it is, then the music is receiving attention rather than the play. For this reason you must make your selections carefully.

3. Background music should be used to heighten the mood of the scene.

4. Music should fade in and out, not snap on and off.

Sound Effects

A poor sound effect will make the audience laugh and destroy the moment of the play. Do as many sound effects "live" as possible. The sound is better and timing can be handled much easier than relying on a record. If you use tape be sure to use colored "leader" between each sound effect.

Hints:

1. I have yet to find a good record of a car starting or stopping, so usually just ignore that sound when it occurs in a play.

2. Many scripts will advertise sound effect records made for that particular play. Save your money. There may be a good one, but all I have purchased have been useless.

3. Try to place telephone bells on stage near the phone or in the foot lights.

4. A large thin metal sheet ($2\frac{1}{2}$ × 5' approximately) hung so that it will swing free is an excellent "thunder sheet." Holding it at the bottom and shaking it gently will cause a good rumble—a hit with a padded mallet or drumstick will give a good crash.

5. A gunshot may be made by smacking or slamming a wide board on the floor. Hold the board at a 45° angle to the floor, place one foot at about the center of the board and on the cue press and let go of the board. Another method, but not so sure is to burst a paper bag. For a series of explosions have all available hands bursting paper bags; the effect is excellent.

Technical rehearsal. If possible you will want to have a technical rehearsal. You may wish to use actors at this rehearsal to let them use the set, but keep in mind that this rehearsal is for the staff. Their problems and adjustments should be considered first.

Dress rehearsal. A dress rehearsal should be exactly like a performance except there is no audience. A dress rehearsal should not be stopped to correct or improve except in extreme emergency. It is a time for actors and staff to have the security of doing the show completely without interruption and making the necessary adjustments if there is an error.

Curtain Call

The bow at the end of the performance is a time when many good amateur productions suddenly look amateurish. The curtain call should be rehearsed along with the rest of the play at least one week before performance. To avoid having any one student receive more (or less) applause than another I preferred to have them all on stage together. While the curtain is down have them return on stage as quickly as possible from the most convenient entrance. They should establish a definite order and be in the same position at each curtain call. As the last person is about to get into position give the cue for the curtain to rise. When the curtain is about three feet over the heads of the actors they may bow to the audience. If the actors take the cue from the center actor the bow can be done almost simultaneously.

EPILOGUE

This portion is devoted to questions asked me by teachers about this method. Probably the answers are all covered in the book, but since these are real questions it seemed a good idea to include both questions and answers. If you want to use this section as a test of your understanding of the drama method, answer the questions before reading the answers. It might interest you to know that these questions came from both native and nonnative speakers of English from Hong Kong, India, Japan, Laos, Philippines, Singapore, Taiwan, Thailand, Iraq, and the U.S.

1. Should we correct the play to put it into "standard" English?

No. First, there is no standard English. The theory of a standard English is disappearing. Generally, the way the language is spoken at the capital of the country is considered the standard. This is not true of the U.S. Second, the play shows us how people talk often with various accents shown. By learning to comprehend these, we understand language and culture better.

2. What about correcting grammatical mistakes that are in the script?

No. People do not always speak grammatically correct. Certainly you will want to use the incorrect grammar to point out what would be correct. Culturally, the incorrect grammar may be important, too. I know of a young Chinese cook who is on his way to becoming a T.V. star in the U.S. with his cooking lessons. His grammar is often incorrect, and his pronunciation is humorous, but his communication to his audience is tremendous. In time he may speak grammatically correct and pronounce perfectly, but he is expressing himself and the audience is interested in him and what he is doing.

3. Do you think the moral implications in some scripts are suitable for high school seniors and college freshmen?

This probably needs to be answered by each teacher. If the situation in the script would be difficult or embarrassing for the teacher to discuss, then another play should be used. There are points that should be considered, however. Probably in most cultures the students are more liberal in their thinking, and know much more than their teachers think they know. Secondly, a moral problem in one culture may not be a moral problem in Western culture. We must not ignore these situations for they are important keys to culture learning. Thirdly, American movies are shown in many countries and the students have already been exposed to many of the situations which may be considered objectional. This question has been asked in relation to a discussion of kissing in a play. In the U.S. we often see people kissing in public. We are a kissing people, but in some cultures it is only part of sex play.

4. Shouldn't we look at the audience sometimes?

Yes, if the script says to talk to the audience. Usually this only happens when there is a narrator or actor stage manager in the play. In most cases the answer is "No." Your eyes should look where you would normally look in the situation. The focus should remain within the framework of the set (real or imagined). Always remember that you are talking to the people on stage. This does not mean that you cannot stand in such a way that your voice will carry to the audience. See the section on stage movement.

5. Can I have girls play men's roles?

Now here's a tricky question. Magic "if" demands that I answer "yes," but this is a situation that is usually embarrassing to all concerned and causes students to behave in an unnatural way. Therefore, avoid it if you possibly can. Another reason concerns the audience more than the actors, for the audience will never believe or accept the play. Of course, the same is true of boys playing women's roles.

6. Can we rewrite plays? Can we add or cut lines and characters?

Yes. If you are using the play in the classroom for language learning you may do just about anything you wish to the play. However, avoid upsetting the story line and check that the behavior remains normal in the situation.

If you are presenting the play to the public and paying royalty you may still make changes that are necessary, such as changing a role from one sex to another or shortening the play. Occasionally a playwright might make a note that nothing may be changed, but this is rare. Again when you make a change, don't let it "destroy" the play.

The seven plays in this book may all be changed and added to as you see fit for classroom or public performance.

7. Why do you feel that students should know each other's names?

It helps establish a group feeling and we are more comfortable with people we know. We arrive at a relaxed atmosphere quicker if we start off by learning names.

8. Why do you have them introduce each other?

It's the best way for them to learn each other's names and for me to be sure they know the names. It is practice in English, and an opportunity to speak in front of others. It is useful English for surely they will find it necessary to introduce someone in English at some future time.

9. You said students felt foolish speaking English. I would think they would be proud. On subways I've heard them talking in English very loudly. Were they with Americans at the time?
Yes.

Then they had a reason to speak in English; they had an excuse to show off perhaps. But students alone speaking in a foreign language is strange. Others around them will most likely react differently towards them and possibly become somewhat annoyed. To speak in a foreign language in your own country, without a special reason, is understandably strange.

10. Why do you want them to form groups?

Most of the students have been working on the language as individuals. With strong motivation this is fine, but many of them feel inadequate and that they cannot succeed. If it becomes a group effort, it seems possible. I expect a great deal of peer teaching to take place. In Japan one must belong to a group—family, school, company, etc. Things are accomplished by groups. If a language class fails to provide a group feeling, it will disintegrate and little language learning will take place.

11. I don't understand why you use "high" and "low" or fast and slow voices with "talk-and-listen" cards?

To get the student to discover what happens with different tones and speeds, and how feeling is often changed. Also to aid him or her to use the varieties of voice control that are used in their own language, that might be helpful in English.

12. Do you use "talk-and-listen" cards even when you are working on a play?

Yes, the cards make it easier for the students to learn the "talk-and-listen" system. Also, they discover that they learn their lines this way. Once they get the hang of it, it's very easy to use the system when working

146

on the play. Remember, of course, the play will progress much slower at the early stages of rehearsal.

13. Don't you think that to use the drama method a great deal depends on the teacher?

I certainly do. A great deal depends on the teacher no matter which method is used.

14. I mean, you seem to have the personality for it. Don't you need a special personality?

Everyone has a special personality. Good teachers must use *their* personalities and use the method and materials the way that suits them best to get their message across. Every method has its specialists. It would be very sad, or even disastrous, if teachers took such a negative attitude about teaching other methods.

15. Must a teacher have drama training?

Proper drama training certainly would be a help, but it's not necessary. I feel enough basics are in the book to help a teacher use the drama method successfully. The drama method involves much more than presenting a play. Most of these can be handled easily by anyone. I feel a drama class would be helpful for everyone, especially teachers and I would like to see it included in all teaching curricula.

16. You used the term "proper drama training," just what did you mean?

I suppose each drama coach or teacher must feel their method is best. I feel that certain methods are not helpful to language learning. Actually any drama training would make one aware of theatre, the relationships between audience and actor, and the many technical aspects of acting and the stage. Certainly this would be a help.

17. Would you be more specific about methods that are not helpful to language learning?

There are directors who insist on actors memorizing their roles before the first rehearsal. This may work for native speakers who are extremely good actors, but I feel it is disaster for the foreign language learner. It is sure to sound memorized and be void of life and true communication. (The same thing happens to most amateur native speakers, too.) Some directors tell their actors exactly how to say their lines, what gesture to use and how to move. This may seem to give security to the language learner, but it is only secure for that line and that situation. Basically, they are not secure for they are copying, not *doing* it themselves. The interpretation is that of the director. In reality people do not express

147

emotion in the same ways, nor do they all speak identically. The students following this method miss out on discovering for themselves and finding the greater security of expressing their own feeling in a new language.

18. In my English conversation class I have sixty students. How can I use your techniques?

I do not think you can teach English conversation to sixty students. Perhaps it's ridiculous for me to say this because you have the situation and you want answers. However, if we all keep pounding away, maybe one day administrators, ministers of education or the Big Boys, whoever they are, will listen.

Now to help you. I would use breathing, lip and tongue and relaxation exercises. If noise levels are no problem, I would add voice exercises. Have several demonstrations of "talk and listen" cards, and then divide the class into groups and have them work by themselves. You could move from group to group to help.

A somewhat similar method could be used with improvisations. After a demonstration, give a new improvisation and have each group work on it and then present it to the class. As they improve, give them more difficult situations letting each group prepare its half or part of an improvisation. Each group would then prepare suitable lines to fit their idea of how the situation should proceed. Of course, once they are performing with another group they must adapt and fit the lines to the responses given them.

Have students bring in objects, and rather than describe the object they should answer questions asked by other students about the object. Such questions as:

What is it?	How much did it cost?
What is it made of?	Could it be used for something else?
What color is it?	Where did you get it? etc.

You might also try a full class improvisation. Situations such as at the airport, train station, hotel, or bazaar are suitable for these. One group of students would be the people employed at such a location and another group would be the people utilizing the area. Give the students preparation time to decide who they wish to be and to set up their necessary area. The entire class will be talking at once when you start. Allow them to move about freely doing what would be natural. You may move about the room acting as an "interpreter" to help out in any difficult situation.

You may also wish to try this as if it were on television. With your "camera," move in on a group. As you move in on the group all other groups stop talking and listen to the group "on camera." Stay with this group as long as you wish then move to another group.

19. Should I keep the groups permanent?

I suppose you might want to test this, but my feeling is "no." This is mainly to avoid competitiveness and to keep a few students from dominating a group. The ideal is to have the entire class become a group, and to make the English class a pleasant experience which students are eager to attend. By working with a number of students, students find security in themselves and in the large group.

20. When we do improvisations should I let them be Japanese speaking English?

Yes, if it is a situation where a Japanese speaks English. This is a fairly rare situation in Japan, however, and therefore, needs to be justified. You might have them be English-speaking people in a Japanese situation. This would have excellent cultural value too, for they must think about their own culture and see it from a tourist's eyes.

Once I asked a group of advanced students how they had used English during the week. The most novel answer came from a lady. One day she lost her train ticket, which she needed in order to leave the station. She was in a hurry and did not want to wait at the Adjustment Office, so she chose to pretend to be an American. When the ticket collector asked for her ticket she looked puzzled and explained her situation in English. The collector understood nothing and, rather than hold up the line, passed her through. The Japanese are very kind and patient with tourists. This is a pretty long introduction to another possibility for a situation where students may speak English in a native situation. Students could be put in many situations where they were pretending to be Americans.

21. If they are pretending, then aren't they "play acting" or not being themselves?

No, they are being themselves pretending. Thus, they must behave as they would behave if they were pretending. They must not pretend to pretend, but pretend.

22. Should we teach British English or American English?

Perhaps the best answer to this was given by Mrs. Mayuri Sukwiwat, Director of the English Language Centre in Bangkok, when she was asked the same question by her nonnative English-speaking teachers, "Why you teach *Thai* English. What else can you teach?" In Japan most students are learning American English, but naturally with a Japanese accent. Since there are so many good British plays, students are often tempted to add a British accent. My advice to them and to you is to have them speak the best English they can. If it's British English fine. If by chance some speak one accent and others another, fine. The point is to be understood, and to communicate to the other actors and to the audi-

149

ence. In some cases you may add a touch of an accent (a broad "a" in a few key words) but generally don't add an accent on an accent.

ROYALTY PAYMENT

Preceeding each published play you will usually find a copyright notice, warning you that you must have permission to perform the play and also pay the required fee. This warning does *not* apply to using the play as a textbook in your classroom for language learning.

Dramatists Play Service states in their catalogue:

> "School Assembly Performances. If the instructor writes us 30 days in advance, we can usually authorize use of most of our one-act plays for assembly, without payment of royalty fees, if these are offered free of charge to student and faculty only, during school hours, and provided no printed publicity is given out. Our plays may also be produced in class-rooms as part of class work as long as no one but students and instructors are present. Again no fee required."

I have found that the other major publisher of plays, Samuel French, is also very understanding and helpful. This is especially true since you are using the play to teach English.

If you should decide to present your play under conditions other than those stated above, and feel the royalty payment would be a hardship, write to the copyright owner, give the following information: (1) why you are presenting the play, (2) date, (3) where the performance will be held, (4) expected attendance, (5) admission charge (in U.S. dollar equivalent), and then ask for reduced or suspended royalty payment.

The royalty payments are not high—most of the one-act plays are in the $5 to $10 bracket. This amount will not be difficult to raise, and since it's the source of a playwright's income, I urge you to comply with the copyright laws.

The following is an example of a letter—

Dramatists Play Service
440 Park Avenue, South
New York, N.Y.

DEAR SIR:

The English-as-a-foreign-language class of Omiya Junior High School has been using *People in the Wind* to study English conversation.

The students are now interested in performing the play for their parents and friends, and would like to get permission to perform it free of royalty.

We hope to perform on November 22nd in our school gymnasium. There will be no admission charge and we expect about one hundred and fifty people.

Any consideration you can give us would be greatly appreciated.

Sincerely yours,

CHIEKO TAKAJIMA
English Instructor
Omiya Junior High School

When you order a number of copies of the same play from any source, always state that you do not intend to produce the play, but will be using it for class work. Most concerns will assume, since you are buying "acting editions," that you are planning a performance, and will, therefore, inform the copyright owners. A simple note on your original order will save unnecessary letter writing later.

I have read all of the plays on the following list and feel that they are all suitable for teaching English. This in no way means that these are the only acceptable plays or that every play on the list will be suitable for every group.

The synopses are brief to give you an idea about the subject matter of the play. Before choosing a play for use I would suggest ordering a single copy of several plays and making a final selection after reading them.

When ordering a play be sure to give the title and the playwright. Titles cannot be copyrighted so there may be several plays using the same title.

The plays marked with * have been used by me or others with successful results. A double ** means the play is highly recommended. At the conclusion of each synopsis I have the publisher—D.P.S.—(Dramatists Play Service) and S.F.—(Samuel French); the cost of the acting edition of the script and the royalty fee in case you plan a public performance.

Where two royalty figures are given the first figure is for the first performance and the second for each subsequent performance.

Do not be overly concerned if a child is listed in the cast. I have used university students to play ten-year-olds on many occasions. Follow the rules of good acting to help the students find the "child" in themselves.

There is no set length for a play, and performing time may vary greatly with each group. A one-act play generally takes about thirty minutes to perform. A three-act or full-length play usually means a playing time of two hours.

Several of the plays have been noted as suitable for mature or advanced groups. "Advanced" means for advanced students of English. "Mature" means that the subject matter is more suitable for university-level students.

All plays and books on drama and theatre may be purchased from The Drama Book Shop. They give excellent service usually shipping the day they receive an order.

Drama Book Shop
150 West 52nd Street
New York, NY 10019 U.S.A.

Plays, of course, may be ordered from the publisher. All correspondence concerning royalty fees must be sent directly to them.

Dramatists Play Service, Inc.
440 Park Avenue South
New York, NY 10016 U.S.A.

Samuel French Inc.
25 West 45th Street
New York, NY 10036 U.S.A.
or
7623 Sunset Boulevard
Hollywood, California 90046
or
27 Grenville Street
Toronto 5, Canada

ONE-ACT PLAYS

An Evening for Merlin Finch*   Charles Dizeno   4 men, 2 women

This funny and imaginative play offers an incisive caricature of family life in the suburbs. The story deals with the problems between father and son, as well as mother and grandmother. (The son and grandmother are played by the same actor—the grandmother exists in the mother's imagination.) There is no plot to speak of, but a lot of funny and unusual stage business, stylish humor and control of language. The "language control" may be a problem for many students since it represents an idea of "mod talk" or people trying to be "in." The last section of the play turns to very normal conversation.

Recommended for advanced groups.

Note: Darlene's mother should be highly exaggerated.

D.P.S., 75¢, $15.00

Bald Soprano*   Eugene Ionesco   3 men, 3 women

A humorous satire on the drabness of the English middle class, in which people fail to understand each other, and get nowhere in their attempt to communicate. For advanced groups.

S.F., $1.95 (in *Four Plays* by Ionesco), $15–$10

Balloon Shot*   Joe Manchester   6 men

A short comedy about an implausible convict whose tall tales of bizzare prison escapes are getting on his cellmates' nerves. Until the wildest story of all comes true.

D.P.S., 75¢, $10.00

The Bespoke Overcoat   Wolf Mankowitz   4 men

Fender, an old Jewish shipping clerk, dies before his friend can make him his first good overcoat. He has waited all his life for such a coat, and returns after dying to visit his friend and remembers some of his life.

The play is easy to stage, but is written with a Jewish rhythm.

S.F. 75¢, $1.50 (in *5 One Act Plays* by Wolf Mankowitz) $10.00

The Browning Version   Terence Rattigan (long one-act)   5 men, 2 women

Concerns a professor at a boys' school who impresses his wife as an academic nincompoop, and who has the reputation among his colleagues of being dull and stodgy and among his pupils of being a ridiculous old stick-in-the-mud. He was none of these things, originally, but circumstances have made him such. The fact that his wife plays around with a younger instructor, and that the headmaster passes him by at the commencement exercises, is deeply humiliating; but the cruelest blow of all is realized that he was perhaps tricked into sympathy by one of his students, and then mocked. He manages to regain his dignity and to start again.

S.F., 75¢, (also in *24 One Act Plays*, $2.50), $20.00

Bus Riley's Back in Town*   William Inge   4 men, 2 women
(see *Glory in the Flower*)

Two young former lovers meet again, and reach out to each other over the pain and bitterness of the intervening years. Good dialogue and interesting characters.

D.P.S., $1.75 (in *11 Plays by Inge*), $15.00

The Call   William Inge   2 men

An allegorical play about 2 men. Joe visits his brother Terry in the city and walks up the twenty-two flights carrying his very heavy suitcases because he does not trust elevators. From habit Joe tries to telephone his mother, though she has been dead several years. Finally, he decides he must move into a hotel in order to be comfortable. He picks up his heavy suitcases which are filled with his memories. The play is an interesting variation on the theme of those who move ahead and those who stay behind clinging to the past.

D.P.S., $1.50 (in *Two Short Plays* by William Inge), $15.00

The Dancers   Horton Foote   3 men, 7 women
A shy young boy discovers that his date for a dance is being forced to go with him against her wishes. He goes to a soda fountain where he meets another girl, Mary Catherine, who also lacks confidence. The two are drawn to each other and make plans to go to another dance. They are afraid of not being able to dance well and of not being popular, but find security in each other and go to their first dance confident and happy.

D.P.S., $1.75 (in *A Young Lady of Property*), $15.00

*The Dear Departed**   Stanley Houghton   3 men, 3 women
A clever dramatization of a famous De Maupassant story about a man who pretended he was dead in order to see what his family thought about him.

S.F., 75¢, $5 (no royalties in Canada)

*The Death and Life of Sneaky Fitch***   James L. Rosenberg
10 men, 3 women, plus many extras
A very funny Western. Sneaky refuses to fit into the expected life style of the West. When he gets ill it's decided that the "Doc" should give him something to finish him off. The funeral is a time for celebration until the coffin opens up and Sneaky comes back from the "dead." He then takes over the town until he really dies. The play shows that people behave the way others expect them to.

D.P.S., $2.45 (in *New American Plays*, volume 1)

*The Dream Unwinds**   Neil Harris   4 men, 2 women
Joe returns home after five years wandering about as a transient laborer. Two friends, Mike and Barney, are with him. During all his travels he has built up in his mind a dream of home. As the play progresses his dream slowly comes to pieces. He comes in contact with the past through his sister, his brother, and his girl. When he realizes that he can never escape the enslaving presence of his parents while at home he knows that his dream has unwound. He and his two friends leave without waiting for the return of his parents.

S.F., 75¢, $5.00

Early Frost   Douglass Parkhirst   5 women (one a child)
Two sisters, Hannah and Louise, live in an old house. Hannah has been

considered strange ever since childhood when a missing playmate was thought to have been carried off by gypsies. When the sisters' young niece, Alice, comes for a visit, Hannah insists that she is the missing child. While Alice is playing in the attic she almost discovers the secret of the missing child.

S.F., 75¢, $5.00

Five in Judgment ** Douglas Taylor 7 men, 1 woman

The story is set in a roadside diner in the Midwest. A storm is going on outside while two farmers complain of the hardships of farming. Bill and Sally, who work at the diner, are somewhat happier about their lot in life. Mack and Danny, two boys hitchhiking to California, enter the diner. The farmers, Roy and Paul, are immediately suspicious and resentful of the newcomers, calling them "bums" and telling them to eat and be on their way. The tension in the diner has reached fever pitch, when a news announcement is heard on the radio—the sixteen year old daughter of a nearby farmer has been found murdered and an alarm has been issued for the arrest of two boys, whose description fit those of Mack and Danny. The two boys realize they are in trouble and dash for the door, but the others grab them and tie them up. All of Mack's and Danny's frantic protestations of innocence are met with scorn and derision. The men argue among themselves, some of them ready to hang the boys. As the men are about to beat Mack and Danny, Paul leaps in to protect the boys. This so enrages Roy that he hits Paul with a violence that kills him. Sally manages to get the Sheriff's office on the phone, and is told that the murderer has been found. Mack and Danny are released, as Roy stands aghast, realizing the enormity of what he has done.

D.P.S., 50¢, $10.00

Flattering Word George Kelly 2 men, 3 women

An actor stops by to see his friend Mary and invites her to see his performance. Mary, however, is married to a very strict minister who dislikes theatre. The actor is convinced that everyone likes to be flattered by being told they should be on the stage. He succeeds in his scheme and Mary and her husband go to the theatre.

Note: The play is a little dated, but is well worth updating.

S.F., 75¢, $10.00

Glory in the Flowers ** William Inge 5 men, 2 women (extras possible)

A somewhat different version of *Bus Riley's Back in Town* and with a more positive ending. In this play Jackie finds her dignity and strength and does not give in to Bus' request to "just have a good time". A combination of the two plays is possible with careful editing.

Of the two plays I prefer *Glory in the Flower*.
Available only in reading version in *24 One Act Plays*
D.P.S., $2.50, $15.00

Happy Journey to Camden & Trenton**   Thornton Wilder   3 men,
3 women
   A stage manager plays several small parts and places the chairs to make
the "Car" for Ma and Pa and their two children so they can make the trip
to visit Beulah, their oldest daughter. Loving and funny, with good family
dialogue. The role of Ma is considerably longer than the others, but it is
an excellent play—one of the best.
   Notes: Though the last scene is very serious, the play is a happy play.
Do not fall into the trap of letting the play become heavy. It is just daily
life not a major dramatic event. Also, it is possible to add an extra man as
the gas station attendant.
   S.F., 75¢, $5.00

Hello out There*   William Saroyan   3 men, 2 women
   A young gambler is arrested and jailed in a small Texas town and
charged with rape. He is not guilty, but the only person who believes him
is Ethel, a young girl who cooks for the prisoners. The young man trusts
her and gives her all of his money before a group of townspeople breaks
into the jail. The husband of the lying woman shoots the young man.
   S.F., 75¢, $10.00

Here We Are   Dorothy Parker   1 man, 1 woman
   A bride and groom are on a train enroute to New York for their honeymoon. Conversation is difficult because of their new marital status and
what is said gets misinterpreted and misunderstood. They wonder if maybe
the marriage is a mistake and they have been unwise. Suddenly, they are
arriving in New York and their first argument ends.
   S.F., $2.50 (in *24 One Act Plays*), $20.00

The Hitch Hiker*   Lucille Fletcher   4 men, 8 women
   A ghost story. A young man driving across the U.S. begins to encounter
a strange and inexplicable hitchhiker. His efforts to explain, then avoid,
and finally destroy the strange figure carry him through many episodes.
The play hovers between reality and unreality. It has bits of local color and
place names of the U.S. pop up frequently.
   Free thinking in staging is necessary.
   D.P.S., $1.50 (with *Sorry Wrong Number*), $10.00

Impromptu*   Tad Mosel   2 men, 2 women
   Four actors are waiting on a darkened stage hoping for some clue as

156

to why they are there, and what is expected of them. As the play progresses some discover themselves, perhaps for the first time. It is a mixture of fantasy and truth.

D.P.S., 50¢, $10.00

Interview**   Jean Claude Van Italle   4 men, 4 women
The eight actors play many parts, the stylized movement keeps the action flowing from one scene to the other. Many aspects of American culture are shown in scenes at a cocktail party, gym class, political rally, church confessional, psychiatrist's office, hospital operating room, etc.

Note: It seems much more difficult to do than it is. It is one of the most popular with Japanese students. Try it!

D.P.S., $1.50 (with T.V. and Motel), $25.00

Its Called the Sugar Plum   Israel Horovitz   1 man, 1 woman
Excellent dialogue in a stimulating yet improbable conflict. A student has run over and killed a young man. The fiancee of the dead man arrives and accuses the student. Before they end up in each others arms they quarrel over the amount of space each of them received in the press. The play is a comedy and it is amusing to watch how their instinctive self-concern overcomes the grief of one and the guilt of the other.

D.P.S., 75¢, $15–$25 (also in *First Season*, 4 Plays by I. Horovitz), $1.65

Long Christmas Dinner**   Thornton Wilder   5 men, 7 women
A dinner that goes on for ninety years covering many dinners. We watch the Bayard family as it grows and dies, stays put and moves away. It is a human, tender, and moving play that is appealing and forceful in its daily conversational dialogue. One of the most beautiful plays in the English language.

Note: This is a happy play. The mood of a Christmas dinner is always one of happiness—the family is together and there is lots of good food. When families come together it is natural that sad things will happen or be discussed. Sad memories may be talked about in a relatively easy manner. Keep the spirit of Christmas always about the play and the comedy and drama will emerge stronger.

S.F., 75¢, $10.00

Long Goodbye*   Tennessee Williams   3 men, 2 women, 4 movers
A young man is moving out of his apartment and a friend visits him. As they talk about his past life, his memories which involve his mother and sister "come to life." A good simple play that should not be played as heavy drama.

D.P.S., $1.95 (in *13 Plays by Williams*), $10.00

EPILOGUE

Lord Byron's Love Letters   Tennessee Williams   1 man, 3 women

A sketch of an old woman and her maiden granddaughter who have an old letter which they show to visitors in exchange for contributions. The letter, supposedly written by the poet Byron, was actually written by the old woman's husband. A humorous and touching play.

D.P.S., $1.95 (in *13 Williams Plays*), $10.00

*Memory of Two Mondays***   Arthur Miller   12 men, 2 women
(long one-act)

A plot based upon the year-in year-out routine drudgery of warehouse laborers. The characters are typical of people everywhere who perform such work. The language is good, strong; and the play is concerned with true, if at times, exaggerated, human values. Somewhat Chekhovian in style it provides many good parts from old lecherous men to young college aspirants.

D.P.S., 75¢, $25.00

*The Midnight Caller**   Horton Foote   2 men, 5 women

Three unmarried women, Alma Jean, Cutie and Miss Rowena, have lived in a house together for years, watching the life of the town. Helen Crews, after a disagreement with her mother, also moves in; Helen had been engaged to Harvey Weems, a charming but weak young man, but the two mothers had managed to break off the engagement. Now Harvey, in love with Helen, but not strong enough to defy his mother, comes every night to Helen's window to call her name. Ralph Johnston, an attractive young man, has just moved to town, and takes up residence in the boarding house, where he becomes very much interested in Helen. Thanks to Ralph's love, Helen is at last able to leave the town and go off to marriage and a happy life of her own, while Harvey, the midnight caller, is left behind still calling for her.

D.P.S., 75¢, $15.00

*Mr. Flannery's Ocean***   Lewis John Carlino   2 men, 1 boy,
4 women, 1 girl

Mr. Flannery, a retired seaman, spends his time taking care of the ocean which he "owns." Mrs. Pringle comes to the resort to spend her last years. She and Mr. Flannery do not get on well together at first, but later he "gives" her his ocean for as long as she wants it.

Problem—Some of Mr. Flannery's and Maug's (the maid) dialogue is written with an accent which should be changed.

D.P.S., $1.50 (in same volume with *Objective Case*), $10.00

A Murder   William Inge   2 men, 1 woman

An allegorical play about a man who must pay large sums of money to his landlady and the houseman in order to have privacy. When he opens

158

the bureau drawer he discovers the body of a dead child. The landlady disclaims any knowledge of the child, but admits the man was not responsible. The man decides to leave knowing that he will not find his peace and release. Once he has gone "the body" in the drawer disappears. The play shows us that the dreams, aspirations and hopes of the man were "murdered" when he was a child, and now he is trapped by others who control him.

D.P.S., $1.50 (in same volume with *The Call*), $15.00

Oil Well   Horton Foote   5 men, 3 women

A Texas farmer has always dreamed of striking it rich and giving his wife and children the things they'd never had. At last it seems he's going to have an oil well "come in," and he abandons all of his planting and harvesting. The well is dry, but his wife's love and faith in him do not vanish in his disappointment.

This play gives an opportunity for students to express many feelings and moods.

D.P.S., $1.75, (in *A Young Lady of Property*), $15.00

One Day in the Life of Ivy Dennison*   Stewart Benedict
2 women, 1 man (see note)

The typical day in the life of a New York secretary. The play is full of cliches, and is a commentary on the superficiality and emotional sterility of those who do not think for themselves. Allows for very imaginative staging using many people since the play takes place in many different places. It is possible to add extra dialogue for other actors in scene 2, 3, 5, and 9.

Note: I prefer to use 5 women and 4 men. The roles of Mr. Green and Mr. Choate could be changed to women.

S.F., 75¢, $5.00

People in the Wind**   William Inge   3 men, 5 women (see note)

A mixed group of passengers, all victims of their differing fates arrive at a bus station rest stop in rural Kansas. The two main characters are a rowdy cowboy and the girl he loves, who imagines herself as a talented performer. This excellent short play (15–20 minutes) is the basis for the fine three-act play and movie *Bus Stop*.

Note: The two old ladies may easily be deleted, rewritten as a man and woman or as two men. It is also possible to write in extra characters who are passengers on the bus.

D.P.S., $1.75 (in volume with 11 *other plays by Inge*), $15.00

Portrait of a Madonna   Tennessee Williams   4 men, 2 women

A demented spinster living alone in an apartment imagines she is visited by a former lover and is pregnant. The porter and apartment manager treat her kindly, the elevator boy with humor, and the doctor and nurse efficiently. A well-drawn character study.

D.P.S., $1.95 (in volume of 13 Williams' plays) $10.00

Pullman Car Hiawatha   Thornton Wilder   15 men, 15 women

Play in novel technique without scenery showing a Pullman (sleeping) car in every possible light. The towns through which it is passing are personified; the weather, the hours of the night, the planets are likewise speaking parts as well as the eight passengers whose partial life stories are shown within the car itself.

Note: Many roles have only one speech. It is possible to eliminate some roles or double. A good play for large groups.

S.F., 75¢, $10.00

Queens of France   Thornton Wilder   1 man, 3 women

A greedy lawyer carries on under the cover of his profession a clever hoax in which he extorts money from gullible women by convincing them they are the rightful heir to the throne of France through relationship to the lost Dauphin.

S.F., 75¢, $10.00

The Rats   Agatha Christie   2 men, 2 women

A good, short mystery play by the master of them all. A woman is invited to a party. Later her lover and other guests arrive. They discover that the hosts of the "party" are in Europe. When the other guests leave the lovers discover they are locked in the apartment and also find the woman's second husband—dead. They are trapped like rats.

Note: For mature students since the language and situation are perhaps unsuitable for high school age.

S.F., 75¢, $10.00

Still Life*   Noel Coward   6 men, 5 women

Laura comes into the restaurant of a railroad station with a cinder in her eye. A doctor, who is having a cup of tea between trains removes the cinder and falls in love with Laura, as she does with him. There are subsequent weekly meetings but finally they decide to part, the doctor to accept a post in Johannesburg and Laura to again go back to a circumspect life. At their last meeting they are suddenly joined by a talkative friend of Laura's. There being no opportunity for a final goodbye, Alec takes his train, Laura tries desperately to calm herself, and the friend chatters on.

S.F., 75¢, $15–$10

The Tiny Closet   William Inge   1 man, 3 women

Mr. Newbold, a tidy middle-aged bachelor, is highly upset because

160

someone has recently been tampering with the lock on his closet. To insure its privacy, he always bolts the door with a lock before leaving his room. Mrs. Crosby, the landlady, insists that she had nothing to do with the tampering, but as soon as Mr. Newbold leaves for work, she and the next door neighbor rush to his room to pry open the closet. They discover no dread secret, but to their amazement dozens and dozens of ladies' hats. Meanwhile, Mr. Newbold, suspicious of Mrs. Crosby's behavior regarding the closet, sneaks back into the house, only to discover his closet broken into and his secret dream world shattered.

D.P.S., $1.75 (in volume of 11 plays), $15.00

To Bobolink for Her Spirit   William Inge   3 men, 4 women
A short play about the dedicated autograph hunters who wait outside one of New York's most famous restaurants.

Note: The names of the celebrities will need to be changed unless it is to be a "period play."

D.P.S., $1.75 (volume of 11 one-act plays by Inge), $15.00

27 Wagons Full of Cotton   Tennessee Williams   2 men, 1 woman, Extras (see note)
In three scenes. Jake burns down a cotton processing shop (gin), and forces his wife to say that he had not left the porch of their house. As a result of the fire Jake gets to gin 27 wagons of cotton. While he gins the cotton, Vicarro, who owns the burned gin, takes advantage of Jake's wife with sadistic pleasure. A strong play with William's emotionally packed dialogue. For mature groups only.

Note: The off-stage lines could easily be given to several extras as they move across the stage going to the fire.

D.P.S., $1.95 (in volume with 13 plays by Williams), $10.00

*The Typists**   Murray Schisgal   1 man, 1 woman
When Paul Cunningham reports for work to address postcards for a mail order house, he makes it clear to his fellow worker, Sylvia Payton, that his employment is strictly temporary. Paul, a married man, is studying law at night. Sylvia, the "supervisor" of the two-employee office, has a few dreams herself—mostly of the romantic variety so often indulged in by not so young spinsters. Within the short span of the play, they begin to age and grow gray. While they go on chattering of the important things that have happened to them and of the bright future which will be coming up any day, the futility of their existence becomes increasingly evident. And when they finally dodder off with a friendly "good night" to their unseen employer, we have withnessed a cycle of life complete with the

humor, sadness, self-delusion, and reconciliation which underlie and infuse the human condition.

Each "age" section could be given to different students.

Note: The age changes should be very subtle.

D.P.S., $1.50 (in volume with *The Tiger*), $25.00

The Sandbox**   Edward Albee   3 men, 2 women

A young athlete in swimming trunks is exercising on the beach. A couple, Mommy and Daddy, enter and decide this is the place. Mommy summons a musician on stage and commands him to play. The couple then exit and return carrying the woman's eighty-six-year-old grandmother, and place her in a child's sandbox. They then wait for her to die and cover herself with sand.

The play is unrealistic and may illustrate our individual selfish concerns and approval of ourselves, as well as our indifference toward the aged.

A short and beautiful play.

Note: The play calls for a clarinetist, but my production had a guitarist who composed his own material. Many instruments are suitable and may be used. The role of Mommy should be overdrawn or enlarged reality. Grandma at times may act very childish.

D.P.S., $1.50 (in volume with *Zoo Story*), $10.00

Sorry Wrong Number*   Lucille Fletcher   3 men, 4 women, extras

A mystery, thriller. The story is about a neurotic invalid whose only contact with the world is her phone. One night, because of crossed wires, she overhears a plan for a murder. Soon she realizes that she is the intended victim and frantically she tries to get help.

The one woman is on stage all of the time with other characters appearing in short scenes that are well written, each being distinct and of vital importance.

Allows for very interesting and imaginative staging.

D.P.S., $1.50 (with *The Hitch Hiker*), $10.00

Still Alarm   George S. Kaufman   5 men

This play is included because it is available in a collection of plays and it requires a cast of men. The dialogue is fine, but the behavior in the situation is strange—this is the satirical humor of the play. Though their hotel is on fire everyone remains calm and behaves in his best "drawing room" manner. Even the firemen act this way, and one of them begins to play his violin (any instrument will do as well).

S.F., 75¢ (and in *24 One Act Plays*, $2.50), $5.00

Strains of Triumph   William Inge   5 men, 1 woman

Ben, a college student overhears Ann, his girlfriend, and Tom, his best friend, talk about their new found love of each other. Ann is concerned about Ben and how their love will affect him. Tom says "he'll get over it." They return to the athletic field nearby where a track meet is taking place in which Ben is to participate Realizing that he has been defeated in the game of love, Ben refuses to participate even though his teammates urge him to return to the meet. He joins an old professor on the hill and observes, thus becoming like the old man, an outsider looking on.

D.P.S., $1.75 (in *11 Plays by William Inge*), $15.00

Trees* Israel Horowitz 3 men, 1 woman (girl) and extras

A father and his daughter go into the forest to chop down a Christmas tree. It is a parable both of man's mindless destruction of his environment and of his callousness to other living things—people.

This is a short play with very little movement.

Note: It is intended that the trees represent Blacks, and father and girl Whites. The trees might, however, represent any oppressed group or idea.

D.P.S., 75¢ (with *Leader*), $15.00

Ugly Duckling* A. A. Milne 4 men, 3 women

Since Princess Camilla is considered plain, the king and queen decide to have the beautiful maid Dulcebella impersonate Camilla until her wedding to Prince Simon. Upon hearing how beautiful Camilla is, Prince Simon has his servant Carlo impersonate him. The two shy lovers, Simon and Camilla meet accidently and fall in love. Each looks beautiful to the other. They get married and live happily ever after.

Note: Some of the characters are overdrawn in typical fairy tale fashion and the acting, too, will need to be larger than life.

S.F., 75¢ (in volume 24, *One Act Plays*, $2.50), $5.00

Will the Real Jesus Christ Please Stand Up* Malcolm Marmorstein 7 men, 1 woman

The action takes place in a television studio, where five actors assemble to read for the role of Jesus in a T.V. spectacular. Four actors give such a poor audition that the discouraged director sends the fifth away without a hearing. The actor accepts this with the silent good grace which he has shown throughout the play. There is meaning in the gentle smile as he leaves.

Note: Because this is well written with interesting characters, it should not be avoided as a "church basement" type play.

D.P.S., 75¢, $10.00

Women Must Weep** Mary Orr 7 women

An absorbing study of the women left behind by fathers, husbands and sons who have gone off to fight in the U.S. Civil War.

D.P.S., $1.50 (with *Women Must Work*), $10.00

Yes Means No*   Howard Emmett Rogers   3 men, 2 women

A very simple play. Teddy tells his father he wants to marry Edith and needs money for his honeymoon. The father accuses his son of having no business sense, having never learned to say "no" to customers wanting easy credit. Father agrees to give Ted $100 every time he says "no" during lunch hour. Ted succeeds in saying "no" many times, often at the wrong time. But all ends well and Ted gets his money for the honeymoon.

Note: Acting can be exaggerated since this is a farce.

D.P.S., 50¢, $5.00

A Young Lady of Property**   Horton Foote   3 men, 6 women

Wilma, a lonely girl of fifteen, lives with her aunt. Her mother is dead, and her father, who is weak and not too reliable, goes around with Mrs. Leighton, a woman of whom the town disapproves. Wilma confesses to her best friend that in a few years she would like to marry and live in the house, which she owns and is her whole identity. Her dream is shattered when she learns that her father plans to marry Mrs. Leighton, and sell Wilma's house. She realizes the only person who can help her now is Mrs. Leighton. To her great joy she discovers that Mrs. Leighton is a person of warmth and sympathy. She saves Wilma's house for her and helps her realize that her father has a right to marry again. Wilma has her house to fill with life so that she need never be lonely.

D.P.S., $1.75 (in *A Young Lady of Property—Six Short Plays*), $15.00

The Zoo Story**   Edward Albee   2 men

A man sits peacefully reading in the sunlight in Central Park. A second man enters, the antithesis of the first. He is a young, unkempt and an undisciplined vagrant, where the first is neat, ordered, well-to-do, and conventional. The vagrant needs to communicate so fiercely that, when he does make the attempt, he alternately frightens and repels his listener. With ironic humor and unrelented suspense we see the young man slowly but relentlessly bring his victim down to his own level and initiate a shocking and horrible ending.

This is probably the best known play by Mr. Albee.

For advanced groups.

D.P.S., $1.50 (in volume with *Sandbox*) $25.00

THREE-ACT OR LONG PLAYS

Ah Wilderness**   Eugene O'Neill   9 men, 6 women

Story of an ordinary family in a small town at the turn of the century. Richard, the high school son who is somewhat of a rebel, is in love with a neighbor's daughter. Trouble starts when the girls' father finds some of

EPILOGUE

the poetry Richard has sent her. He forbids the girl to meet the boy. Richard is crushed and goes to a bar and gets drunk, but the girl sneaks away and meets him at the beach and we know everything will work out.

The play is beautifully written, humorous and tender, with great understanding of all of the characters.

Note: The script calls for four sets, however, I feel it is quite easy to combine the living room-dining room area into a single or divided set. The other two sets may be quite small possibly using down stage left and right.

This play is available in many libraries.

S.F., $1.50, $50–$25

Anastasia   Guy Bolton (adapted from the play by Marcelle Maurette)
8 men, 5 women

Beunine finds a girl who seems to be the missing Anastasia, perhaps the only member of the imperial family of Russia who survived the massacre. If he can prove she is Anastasia she will receive a huge fortune being held in an English bank, and he will get his share. Success is almost certain, but the girl must face the imperial grandmother for final acceptance. The meeting is a beautiful piece of theatre, and is often done by young actresses in acting classes. The play ends with the audience believing the girl is the real Anastasia, but she decides to spurn the money, her sordid associates, and return to her true love and simple life.

S.F., $1.50, $50–$25

Anniversary Waltz   Jerome Chodorov and Joseph Fields
7 men, 5 women

On their fifteenth wedding anniversary the husband makes a wine-inspired mistake—he tells his in-laws about his romancing with his wife before they were married. Problems mount, tempers rise, until everything explodes. However, the play ends on a warm and tender note and the family has gained an understanding of each other. A human and funny play.

D.P.S., $1.50, $50–$25

*Arsenic and Old Lace***   Joseph Kesselring   11 men, 3 women

Two charming and innocent little old ladies provide a home and final resting place for lonely men with no reason to live. They help the men "escape" this dreary world and bury them in the basement of their home. This very funny comedy also introduces us to their brother who thinks he is Teddy Roosevelt and another younger brother, a newspaperman, who uncovers the activities of the household.

D.P.S.,$1.50, $35–$25

EPILOGUE

Blithe Spirit   Noel Coward   2 men, 5 women

Sophisticated! Charles and his second wife, to entertain friends, invite a medium to hold a seance. The spirit that returns turns out to be Charles first wife who begins to cause a great deal of mischief. The first wife decides to have Charles "join" her and "fixes" the car, but the second wife is the one who takes the fatal automobile ride. Both ladies then return to plague Charles. He manages, however to extricate himself.

S.F., $1.50, $50–$25

Bus Stop**   William Inge   5 men, 3 women

A small group of passengers, on a bus going to Wichita, is forced to spend the night in a small restaurant because of a storm. One of the passengers is a rather untalented nightclub performer who is being pursued by a very determined young cowboy. Others are a drunken professor who is trying to run away from his past, a fatherly cowboy who is traveling with the young cowboy, and the bus driver who becomes friendly with Grace the restaurant owner. By morning all of the problems have been solved, the storm has subsided, and the bus moves on. It is a play full of humor, compassion, and appreciation of average humanity.

D.P.S., $1.50, $50–$25

Come Back Little Sheba*   William Inge   8 men, 3 women

"Doc" was forced to give up his study of medicine and marry Lola because he had had an affair with her. With all of his hopes gone he settled down to a dull life with the tedious woman and became an alcoholic. It is the story of the deep seated frustration in their marriage and its inevitable and furious eruption.

S.F., $1.50, $50–$25

The Corn Is Green   Emlyn Williams   10 men, 5 women, extras

An English spinster opens a school in a Welsh mining town. One student shows outstanding ability and the teacher is determined to help him in every way possible. The boy, overworked studying for a scholarship, suddenly rebels against help from the woman and succumbs to the charms of a flashy young girl. The teacher's courage and wisdom finally brings the boy back to his senses. He wins the scholarship and the teacher continues her school with the added responsibility of taking care of the child of the girl and boy.

Very difficult Welsh words are used at times, but there is a very helpful pronunciation chart included.

The play is particularly well suited for teaching English as that is part of the play.

D.P.S., $1.50, $35–$25

EPILOGUE

The Curious Savage**   John Patrick   5 men, 6 women

Mrs. Savage a rich widow wants to give her money away to worthy people who need to be foolish, rather than to foolish people with worthy ideas. Her stepchildren declare her insane so as to get the money. Unfortunately, once they have her in a home for the mentally disturbed they cannot find the money. Mrs. Savage finds the people "inside" are not as "insane" as those "outside." The dominant mood is comedy and one is left with the feeling that the virtue of kindness and affection have not been entirely lost in a world that seems to be motivated by greed and dishonesty.

D.P.S., $1.50, $35–$25

The Dark at the Top of the Stairs   William Inge   6 men, 4 women

The plot is less one story than a series of short stories—the fight between a husband and wife; the fear of a shy girl going to a dance; the problems of an introverted little boy; the corroding marriage of the wife's rowdy sister; and the tragedy of a young Jewish cadet.

Mr. Inge is saying that there is dark at the top of everyone's stairs, but that it can be dissipated by understanding, tolerance, compassion and love.

D.P.S., $1.50, $50–$25

Death of a Salesman**   Arthur Miller   8 men, 5 women

Willie Loman, a salesman, has come to the end of the line. He has built his life on false values, and has nothing to give him courage, only his wife remains absolutely true. He goes through a series of soul-searching revelations to try and discover where he failed to win success and happiness. He finally decides that his death would at least give his family insurance money which would give them happiness. Thus, even his death is related to his false idea of what brings happiness. The death also causes one son to try to prove his father right and we know the same mistake will be repeated. A very powerful play for advanced students. Unit set needed.

D.P.S., $1.50, $50–$25

The Desk Set   William Marchant   8 men, 8 women

A woman full of facts and figures works in the reference department of a television network. An efficiency expert begins replacing the humans with machines with mechanical brains. The mechanical brains are no match, however, for the clever woman. There is a romance running throughout the play and a little heartache.

S.F., $1.50, $50–$25

167

EPILOGUE

The Diary of Anne Frank**   A dramatization by Frances Goodrich and Albert Hackett of the book, *Anne Frank: The Diary of a Young Girl* by Anne Frank   5 men, 5 women

Winner of the Pulitzer Prize and Critics Circle Award. A play full of humor, warmth, beauty, gentle pity, and hope. The story of a group of Jewish people who hide in an attic during German occupation.

D.P.S., $1.50, $50–$25

Father of the Bride   Caroline Francke based this play on the novel by Edward Streeter   11 men, 7 women, extras

About the problems the father of a bride must face when the small wedding planned turns into a big wedding. A funny comedy of family life.

D.P.S., $1.50, $35–$25

The Glass Menagerie**   Tennessee Williams   2 men, 2 women

A drama of great tenderness, gentle humor, and beauty. I feel it is Mr. Williams' best.

Amanda, a faded beauty of a more genteel life, lives with her son, Tom, and slightly crippled daughter, Laura, in a dingy apartment. She tries to improve and give meaning to their lives, but her methods are ineffective. Amanda's constant nagging at Tom drives him to escape in the unreal world of the movies and causes Laura to keep to herself with her glass collection. Amanda finally persuades Tom to bring a friend from work to meet Laura. The young man, Jim, turns out to be engaged and all of the work and efforts to entrap him are for naught. The world of illusion they have created crumbles. Tom, like his father, leaves home; but he cannot erase the memory of Laura from his mind.

D.P.S., $1.50, $50–$25

Goodbye My Fancy   Fay Kanin   8 men, 12 women

A liberal Congresswoman returns to her school with a film depicting the horrors of war. The film is considered harsh and improper by the trustees, and the Congresswoman realizes that her former lover, who is now president of the school, is a spineless person. She turns then to a photographer who has come to cover her lecture and film.

Note: The references to the war will need to be updated.

S.F., $1.50, $50–$25

I Remember Mama**   John Van Druten   9 men, 13 women

This heartwarming study of American life shows how Mama brings up her family in San Francisco during the early years of the century giving them security with her strength, common sense and nonexistent bank account. Highly recommended.

168

EPILOGUE

Note: Request the "High School Version." Many sets are suggested, however, it may be performed on a unit set or virtually bare stage. I used a back wall to represent the kitchen which stayed on stage throughout. The downstage areas right and left were used for all other scenes.

D.P.S., $1.50, $25

*Lovers and Other Strangers** 5 men, 5 women

Four one-act comedies dealing with the problems of love and marriage. One shows the awkward behavior of a young man when he invites a girl to his apartment; another about a young man who stops by his fiancee's apartment at 3 A.M. to tell her the wedding is off. The third (for mature groups) concerns dominance in bed and its relationship to the office. The fourth, the most serious, and thus, the most amusing shows a mother and father desperately trying to save their son's marriage which is breaking up. We learn very little about the son's marriage, but a great deal about the parents'.

For mature groups.

S.F., $1.50, $50–$25

The Male Animal James Thurber and Elliot Nugent 8 men, 5 women

Tommy, a quiet professor at a midwestern university, has been married for ten years. Joe, who was a great football star, returns to Tommy's school for a big game. At one time, he was unofficially engaged to Tom's wife, Ellen. To add to this problem one of his students has written an inflammatory article for the school magazine, and Tom has a good chance of being fired if he reads a letter by Vanzetti to his class—the trustees are shouting "red" so loud they cannot hear ideas. Ellen begs Tommy not to read the letter. Tommy challenges Joe to a fight and makes a firm stand on reading the letter to uphold the principal of freedom of ideas. Ellen now realizes that he is a good example of the male animal and backs him up.

S.F., $1.50, $50–$25

The Mousetrap Agatha Christie 5 men, 3 women

Perhaps the longest running play in the world—a distinction it hardly deserves.

In standard mystery form a group of strangers are stranded in a boarding house during a storm. One of them is later murdered. Into this group comes a policeman, traveling on skis, and soon there is another murder. The policeman begins to probe and question everyone, but in a switch it is the policeman or the man disguised as a policeman who is the killer.

S.F., $1.50, $50–$25

169

EPILOGUE

My Sister Eileen*   Joseph Fields and Jerome Chodorov   21 men, 6 women, extras. Some parts may be doubled or be cut.

This humorous play deals with the adventures of two sisters who come to New York from a small town in Ohio. The apartment they rent in Greenwich Village has a flow of visitors—drunks, cops, hustlers, muscle men, sailors, etc.

    D.P.S., $1.50, $25

My Three Angels   Sam and Bella Spewack   7 men, 3 women

The scene is French Guiana where three convicts are hired to repair the roof of a home. Papa is about to lose his business to his hard cousin. A cold-blooded nephew who is traveling with the cousin decides to jilt Papa's daughter for an heiress. The "three angels" step in and solve all of Papa's problems in their own way. They have warm hearts, clever hands, thinking brains, and employ every criminal art to do their job. A very funny play.

    D.P.S., $1.50, $50–$25

The Odd Couple   Neil Simon   6 men, 2 women

Felix has left his wife and moved in with Oscar who left his wife sometime ago. Felix is neat and orderly while Oscar is just the opposite. The patterns that broke up their marriages begin to appear in this new "marriage" with very funny results. Four friends, who come in to play poker, are well drawn characters as are the two young English girls who live upstairs. An extremely funny play.

    S.F., $1.50, $50–$35

Our Town**   Thornton Wilder   17 men, 7 women
(doubling possible in small roles)

A real American classic that has been performed around the world. Just about everyone can identify with and understand this beautiful play. Certainly my first choice.

The play is set in a small town in New Hampshire and shows us the life of the people. The first act is called "Daily Life"; the second "Love and Marriage"; and the third is untitled—you can guess what its about.

Mr. Wilder says "[Our Town] is an attempt to find a value above all price for the smallest events in our daily life. . . . Our claim, our hope, our despair are in the mind—not in things, not in 'scenery'."

Indeed the only scenery and props needed are two tables, some chairs, two ladders, and two trellises. On a suggestion from Mr. Wilder's notes I used human voices for *all* sound effects. It added greatly to the humanness of the play and was much easier to control.

    S.F., $1.50, $25–$25

Also available at 65¢ from A Perennial Classic, Harper and Row Publishers, and in many anthologies.

Papa Is All   Patterson Greene   3 men, 3 women
An insight into the family life of the Pennsylvania Dutch. Papa is a tyrant and demands the simple life for his family. The son and daughter think their father is more interested in keeping them on the farm than in following the orthodox Mennonite life. With Mama's help they steal away to see a movie. Papa finds out and goes after the girl and her date. An interesting comedy.
Some of the dialogue is in Pennsylvania Dutch English—such as the title, which means Papa is dead.
S.F., $1.50, $35–$25

Philadephia Here I Come*   Brian Friel   9 men, 4 women
The night before he departs for the U.S., a young Irishman looks over the life he is leaving. His alter ego appears and adds to the humor by tossing out his irreverent thoughts. He says farewell to his father, who cannot communicate with him, his girlfriend, and his pals. We also meet the rather loud and flashy aunt and uncle he will be staying with in Philadelphia. A lovely play.
S.F., $1.50, $50–$25

Picnic**   William Inge   4 men, 7 women
A Pulitzer Prize and Critics Circle Award play.
Into a female atmosphere (a mother, two daughters, three female schoolteachers and a middle-aged neighbor woman) a young virile man arrives and upsets the entire group. One daughter runs off with the young man sacrificing her chance for wealth and marriage, which her mother had hoped for to change their lives. The other daughter grows up as a result of her brief encounter with the young man. One schoolteacher is stirred to make her on-again off-again romance come to a head. An excellent play.
D.P.S., $1.50, $50–$25

The Rainmaker   N. Richard Nash   6 men, 1 woman
Lizzie, the only girl on the farm, is plain and afraid of becoming an old maid. There is a drought in the area and a brash young rainmaker arrives and offers to make it rain for $100. It seems a silly idea, but the family consents. The rainmaker also tries his magic on Lizzie telling her she has a special beauty all her own. Just as her father believes he can bring rain, Lizzie begins to believe she is pretty. Rain does come and so does love to Lizzie.

EPILOGUE

One set with two small acting areas on Right and Left stage.
S.F., $1.50, $50–$25

The Solid Gold Cadillac   Howard Teichmann and George S. Kaufman
11 men, 6 women
   A humorous look at American big business. It shows how a little old lady with ten shares of stock gains control of a corporation by outwitting the "wicked" directors. The directors are all stereotype caricatures and must be played broadly. There are many sets, but they can be simple and stylized to make a production possible. Radio and film sequences can easily be handled as live radio or T.V. broadcasts.
   D.P.S., $1.50, $50–$25

A Streetcar Named Desire   Tennessee Williams   6 men, 6 women
   One of the great plays of American theatre. The play reveals in great depth the character of Blanche, a woman whose life has been undermined by romantic illusions which eventually lead her to reject the realities of life. The pressure brought to bear upon her by her sister with whom she goes to live, and by the sister's earthy and animallike husband leads to her tragic self-delusion and causes her to be sent to an insane asylum. The play shows that brute force will conquer and destroy the weak and sensitive.
   This play is recommended for advanced and mature groups only.
   Note: 2 Men, 2 Women have the major portion of the play.
   D.P.S., $1.50, $50–$25

*Summer and Smoke**   Tennessee Williams   8 men, 6 women
   A somewhat puritanical girl and an unpuritanical young doctor are basically attracted to each other, but because of their differing attitudes toward life they are driven apart. Over the years, however, the young doctor realizes that the girl's high idealism is right, but the girl has now learned to accept the doctor's previous views. Thus, their differing attitudes still keep them apart.
   D.P.S., $1.50, $50–$25

*Tea and Sympathy**   Robert Anderson   9 men, 2 women
   This is the story of a sensitive boy in a boarding school who is teased by his classmates because he played a girl's part in a play. The teasing turns to rumor about him being homosexual. The master of the house joins in the persecution, and the boy's father does not even understand him. To prove his manliness he makes a date with a cheap local girl, but it turns out to be his downfall. He sickens at the sight of her, and returns beginning to doubt himself. The master's wife comes to his rescue and offers him understanding and sympathy.

172

A tender and honest play. The girl does not appear in the play so there are no shocking scenes to be dealt with.
S.F., $1.50, $50–$25

Ten Little Indians   Agatha Christie   8 men, 3 women
A mystery. Eight guests and two servants are invited to a country home for a weekend. They do not know each other nor do they know the host. A mysterious voice accuses each of murdering someone—not a murder that would hold up in court, but murder just the same. There are ten Indian statues on the mantlepiece and when one suddenly tumbles off, almost immediately one of the guests dies of a poisoned drink. As each statue falls another person dies—only two remain alive.
S.F., $1.50, $50–$25

Time of the Cuckoo   Arthur Laurents   5 men, 5 women
The story concerns an American secretary, past her prime and unmarried, who is making her first trip to Europe. She is a warm and forthright person with no complexes, but has a desire for affection. She meets a Venetian shopkeeper who offers her the love she craves, but she is shocked to learn that he is happily married and is not afraid to admit it. She, thus, realizes that there are different views of morality in different cultures, but she cannot accept his love.
Because of the theme, the play is probably suited for mature groups though there is no vulgarity in the play. There is one scene, the climax of the play, where the secretary gets drunk which must be played carefully. It must not be a humorous "stage" drunk.
S.F., $1.50, $50–$25

*The Torchbearers**   George Kelly   6 men, 6 women
A broad spoof on amateur theatricals. The first act is the rehearsal in the living room of one of the members. The second act is the seeming disaster that usually takes place backstage during performances. The third act is back in the living room reliving what has happened.
The second act is extremely funny and is worth doing by itself as a one act play.
S.F., $1.50, $50–$25

*A View from the Bridge**   Arthur Miller   12 men, 3 women
A tragedy showing the destructiveness of jealousy. A longshoreman makes room in his home for two Italian cousins who have been smuggled into the country. One, young and very handsome, falls in love with the young niece living in the same house. The longshoreman who always thought of his niece as a daughter becomes insanely jealous and no one can stop him from causing the tragic conclusion.
D.P.S., $1.50, $50–$25

Years Ago   Ruth Gordon   4 men, 5 women

A true story of Ruth Gordon's teenage years when she fell in love with theatre. Papa wants her to be a physical culture instructor, but Ruth hates the idea. She has an interview with a theatrical manager and Mama helps her confront Papa. Realizing that Ruth has the spunk and determination, Papa gives her his most prized possession—a spy glass—to pawn if she needs money. A nice play showing family life of years ago, and the dialogue is well written and useful.

D.P.S., $1.50, $35–$25

You Can't Take It with You**   Moss Hart and George S. Kaufman
9 men, 7 women, extras

A modern American classic. The Sycamores seem like a mad family. Mother writes, father makes firework displays, one daughter makes candy and studies ballet, another daughter has a regular job, and Grandpa raises snakes and attends graduations. They are a dear and delightful group who attract a number of other interesting people to their home— a banker, tax collector, Russian ballet teacher, a former Grand Duchess, and a drunken actress.

D.P.S., $1.50, $25

COLLECTIONS OF ONE-ACT PLAYS AVAILABLE IN PAPERBACK

24 Favorite One-Act Plays, ed. Bennett Cerf and Van H. Cartmell. Dolphin Books, Doubleday and Co. Inc. Garden City, N.Y. $2.50 Includes: *A Memory of Two Mondays*, *The Browning Version*, *27 Wagons Full of Cotton*, *Glory in the Flower*, *The Happy Journey* and *Sorry Wrong Number*.

Young Lady of Property, Horton Foote
With five other one act plays in an acting edition. Dramatist Play Service. $1.75

One-Act Plays of William Inge
Eleven plays including *To Bobolink For Her Spirit*, *The Tiny Closet*, *People In The Wind*, and *Bus Riley's Back In Town*. Acting edition. Dramatist Play Service. $1.75

The Best Short Plays, edited by Stanley Richards
(formally edited by Margaret Mayorca)
Published yearly and includes fourteen to fifteen plays. Chilton Book Co., Philadelphia, Pa. (1969). $1.95

27 Wagons Full of Cotton, Tennessee Williams
   With 12 other one-act plays, including *Portrait of a Madonna,
   Lord Byron's Love Letters* and *The Long Goodbye.* New Directions.
   $1.95

GLOSSARY

Above	Upstage of; usually behind
Ad lib	Lines or words made up by the actors
Backing	Scenery outside of doors and windows; masking
Back lighting	Lighting behind the general acting area, lighting from upstage
Below	Downstage of; usually in front of
Bit Part	A small role in a play under five lines
Blocking	Stage movements
Border lights	A strip of overhead lights which hangs behind the border curtain
Build	Gradually increase in volume or tempo
Cleat	A metal piece used with a lash rope to fasten scenery flats together
Cover	To stand in front of another actor thus blocking the audience's view of him
Cross	To walk; go: move
Cue	The last three words of the previous actors speech; the signal for stage action such as entrance cue, cue for the telephone
Cues, Pick-up	To start words or actions immediately after previous speaker
Curtain line	The imaginary line where the front curtain hits the stage

Double	To have two actors prepared to play the same role
Dressing	The props used to decorate the set
Extra	A nonspeaking part; could appear in crowd scenes with ad lib lines
False proscenium	The opening created by flats or curtains to make the stage opening smaller. Teasers
Follow spot	A bright spotlight that is manned, used to follow an actor about the stage, generally used in musicals, rarely in plays
Foots	The lights on the apron of the stage; a strip of lights on the floor at the edge of the stage. Rarely used on Broadway except for musicals
Front curtain	The main curtain
Front lights	Any lights for the stage that are placed in front of the procenium arch
In	To move toward center of stage
Indicated acting	To pretend; not truthful; to show the outward manifestation rather than inner feeling
Legs	Stage curtains hung on left and right stage parallel to the footlights. Tormentors
Out	To move away from center stage
Pace	The speed of speaking or moving. "Pick up the pace of that scene." "Slow down the pace."
Pipes	The pipes hung above the stage on which lights and borders are hung
Properties	The objects used on stage by the actors. Furniture and anything that is handled
Scenery	Anything used to denote location of the play
Selvage	The edge of cloth woven so it will not ravel
Set	The scenery
Spot	Spotlight; a lighting unit for the stage. Not to be confused with follow spot
Top	To speak louder than previous speaker

GLOSSARY

Unit Set	An all purpose set used to denote many locations with little or no change
Walk-on	An extra or bit part
Wings	The space off stage right and left

BIBLIOGRAPHY

DRAMA AND EDUCATION

Barnes, Douglas, ed. "Drama in the English Classroom," Champaign, Ill., 1966. (Pamphlet of the National Council of Teachers of English.)

Birke, Gisella. "Creating People Without Faces," *Speech and Drama* 21 (Summer, 1972): 28–30.

Cammack, Floyd M. "Language Learning Via Via," *Journal of English Teaching* 2 (May, 1968): 4–9.

Day, Christopher W. "The Basis, Drama in Colleges of Education," *Speech and Drama* 20 (Summer, 1971): 7–11.

Hauger, George. "Presence and Gesture in Communication," *Speech and Drama* 16 (Spring, 1967): 8–10.

Heathcote, Dorothy. "Drama and Education: Subject or System?" in *Drama and Theatre in Education*, ed. Nigel Dodd and Winifred Hickson. London: Heinemann Educational Books Ltd., 1971

Isenberg, David R. "Drama Without Space," *Speech and Drama* 21 (Summer, 1972): 17–22.

Moffett, James. "Drama: What is Happening," Champaign, Ill., 1967. (Pamphlet of the National Council of Teachers of English.)

Seely, John. "The Language of Improvisation," *Speech and Drama* 20 (Summer, 1971): 2–6.

––––––. "Sincerity, Reality and Fiction," *Speech and Drama* 20 (Autumn, 1971): 11–15.

Sherborne, Veronica. "Movement as a Preparation for Drama," in *Drama and Theatre in Education*, ed. Nigel Dodd and Winifred Hickson. London: Heinemann Educational Books Ltd., 1971.

Styan, J.L. "Drama and the Sensorium," *Speech and Drama* 17 (Spring, 1968): 9–12.

BIBLIOGRAPHY

Via, Richard A. "English Through Drama," *English Teaching Forum* 10 (July-August, 1972): 3–7.

———. "TESL and Creative Drama," *English Teaching Forum* 10 (November-December, 1972): 22–23.

———. "A Lesson in Creative Dramatics" *English Teaching Forum* 11 (June-August, 1973).

ACTING

McGaw, Charles. *Acting Is Believing.* San Francisco, Calif.: Rinehart Press, 1966.
Moore, Sonia. *The Stanislavski System.* New York: Pocket Books, 1967.
Rockwood, Jerome. *The Craftsman of Dionysus.* Glenview, Illinois: Scott Foresman, 1966. (perhaps best for the beginner)
Spolin, Viola. *Improvisations for the Theater.* Evanston, Ill.: Northwestern University Press, 1970.
Stanislavski, Constantin. *An Actor's Handbook*, trans. Elizabeth Reynolds Hapgood. New York: Theatre Arts Books, 1963.
Way, Brian. *Development through Drama.* London: Longmans, 1967.

STAGECRAFT

Adix, Vern. *Theatre Scenecraft.* Children's Theatre Press, 1966. (perhaps best for beginner)
Corson, Richard. *Stage Makeup.* New York: Meredith Publishing Co., 1967. (very detailed)
Hake, Herbert V. *Here's How.* New York: Samuel French, 1958. (simple and handy)
Nelms, Henning. *A Primer of Stagecraft.* New York: Dramatist Play Service, 1955.
Parker, W. Oren and Harvey K. Smith. *Scene Design and Stage Lighting.* New York: Holt, Rinehart and Winston, 1968. (advanced)